SAVING DAD

For mum and dad

Saving Dad
The remarkable true story of a son's battle to save his father from a lifetime of mental illness

Written by Matt Janes
Cover design: Matt Janes
Tear drop illustration: Olga Moonlight/Shutterstock.com
Design and production: Emma Jones
Editor: Fiona Shaw
Proofreader: Lucy Chesters

Printed and bound in Great Britain by Clays Ltd, Elcograf S.p.A

ISBN: 978-1-9160267-2-8

First published in October 2019 by Wordscape Ltd.
Northern Lights Building,
5 Mann Street
Liverpool L8 5AF
wordscape.org.uk

mattjanes.com

SAVING DAD

MATT JANES

A note from the author

Hello.

Thank you for choosing to read my story. ***Saving Dad*** is the true story of my battle to save my father from a lifetime of mental illness. It recounts my personal experience of the ups and downs, as well as the hope and despair of fighting against his illness. In no way does it represent medical advice or claim to provide the answer to anyone else's mental distress. Instead, it is an invitation to explore what's possible.

Along the way, you'll bump into a few words from the world of neuroscience – which, as you'll see, is a complex and fascinating subject. It's also one which I've spent several years studying so, rather than expect you to do the same, I've added a glossary. You'll find it at the back of the book, so that you're not bombarded with a technical explanation mid-story.

Best wishes,

Matt

Prologue

I WAS three years old when I first witnessed the devastating effects of depression.

On a winter's morning in 1975, as I peddled my beloved plastic tricycle into the kitchen, I saw my dad sobbing in mum's arms.

Whilst being cradled, he was repeating the words,

"I can't. I can't."

Although at the time I was too young to understand, the scene I witnessed was dad's first battle with bipolar disorder. Over the years, this mental illness has caused him to cycle between exhilarating highs and the depths of despair.

Until recently, this book didn't have an ending. Since this is the true story of my life, I had to be patient enough for it to write its own.

Recently, it did just that.

Chapter One

TWO years before I was born, mum and dad moved from the south east of England, where they had lived all of their lives, to the north west. Mum was pregnant with my older brother, Stuart, getting prepared for the arrival of her first child.

Dad was also getting prepared, but in a slightly different way. He'd secured an exciting new job with the local water authority. Only, he hadn't told mum about it. And, 'local', as it turned out, wasn't very local.

Approximately 220 miles separates Surrey and the Wirral peninsula, a one-way journey that dad and a shell-shocked mum made in a bright orange Volvo estate, with a screaming newborn baby.

Like most things in life, mum took it in her stride and put complete faith in dad's judgement, trusting that he knew exactly what he was doing.

Two and a half relatively uneventful years later, in September 1972, I was born. This time, there would be no new job and no return journey to the south east of England. All was quiet.

The silence was soon broken by the sound of falling bricks. Mum returned from strolling me around the neighbourhood to the sound of the wall between the kitchen and dining room crashing to the floor. Either dad hadn't wanted to give her the opportunity to oppose his idea for an extended kitchen diner, or once again he had 'forgotten' to tell her of his new plans.

To be fair to him, dad made an exceptional job of the new, enlarged space. To mum, it didn't immediately look as though it would turn out this way, when she saw a lorry unload half an ash tree, complete with bark, onto the drive.

But – once dad had kitted out the garage with an industrial band saw, jigsaw, radial arm saw, lathe, router and sanding plate (without telling the neighbours) – he quite brilliantly transformed the former piece of woodland into a bespoke, handmade kitchen.

As well as being adept at knocking down walls, as a chartered civil engineer, he was well qualified to build them. So build them he did; but not before a 12 hour day at the office. When he arrived home, he would swap his suit for a pair of jeans, then start work on the house. I remember how happy he looked, digging the foundations for the extension by floodlight, long after the sun had gone down.

From their newly-constructed bedroom balcony, mum and dad had a lovely clear view of the Dee Estuary and North Wales. Perhaps it was the sight of the boats sailing by that inspired dad to buy his first yacht. Evidently, he didn't want the boat builder to have all the fun, so – rather than buy one that he could put straight onto the water – he bought a 22-foot-long fibreglass kit.

Now that the ash tree had vacated the drive, there was room for a makeshift boat yard. So, over the next few months, when dad got home from a day's work, rather than build a house extension, he built a boat. To me, all of this seemed perfectly normal, establishing my belief that dad could achieve absolutely anything.

Like with all of his projects, he kitted out the boat to an exceptionally high standard and, once she was ready, we set sail.

Well, I say 'sail'. The boat's first voyage was a two-week holiday in northern Spain, which began on the road.

Out came the trusty Volvo estate, a blue one by now, to trail the newly-built vessel to the Costa Brava and back, a total of 2,200 miles. To dad, this was just another adventure, complete with new boat, wife and two young children. What could possibly go wrong?

He'd already driven the 270 miles down to the south coast, crossed the English Channel from Portsmouth to Cherbourg, then driven another few hundred miles through France, when he fell asleep at the wheel.

It wasn't until we saw the headlights of the juggernaut coming directly for us, that dad woke up and returned us to the right side of the road. Disaster averted. We took this as a sign to stop over for the night, so pulled over into a lay-by.

(The beauty of trailing a boat is that you have ready-made beds wherever and whenever you need them.)

By early daylight, we were back on the road and soon engrossed in a game of 'I spy'. When mum glanced into the passenger wing mirror, she spied 'w' for 'wobbling wheel'. The nuts which secured one of the wheels to the trailer had worked themselves loose and the wheel was coming off its axle. Dad managed to navigate to the hard shoulder, where we came to a stop, before the wheel had a chance to break free.

We quickly jumped out of the car to see how close we had been to another potential accident. "What an adventure!" ten-year-old me thought. The wobbling action had caused the wheel's bolt holes to wear, so now the nuts wouldn't fully tighten. We had no spares and another 600 miles to go before we reached the harbour. I was in awe as I watched dad ingeniously turn the nuts around through 180 degrees, so that their natural shape trapped the wheel in place, nice and securely on the axle.

The holiday passed without further incident and the whole experience reinforced my belief that, whenever there was a problem, dad knew how to fix it. Like many father-son relationships, dad was my idol and I wanted to be just like him.

Through my parents' impetuous move to the north west, I was presented with the relatively rare opportunity to attend grammar school. Where I grew up on the Wirral peninsula, there are four grammar schools within close proximity.

Unfortunately for me, they didn't simply hand out places for an opportunity like that. Instead, you needed to pass the 11-Plus entrance exam.

Up until this point in my life, I can safely say that my experience of anxiety was limited to whether or not Liverpool were going to win the football league trophy. Thanks to Ian Rush and 'King' Kenny Dalglish, I rarely needed to worry about that.

Watching those 11 men in red win title after title filled me with great excitement, whilst the 11-Plus gave me palpitations of a different kind. Even from seven or eight years old, I can remember how this exam hovered on the horizon of my future.

My older brother had already successfully navigated the hurdle to grammar school, heaping further pressure on me to do the same.

The cruel thing about the 11-Plus was that you didn't know when you were going to sit the exam. It would be sprung upon you as a surprise, on what would otherwise be a regular school day.

The anticipation of the impending exam took its toll, as I contracted glandular fever. I don't remember being a practising romantic at the age of 11, but this diagnosis of 'the kissing disease' suggested otherwise.

For a few weeks, I was listless and struggled to get out of bed, which meant missing school.

It also meant missing the 11-Plus.

I remember my friend, Neil, coming to the front door one day to say that they'd sat the exam. I immediately felt a sense of dread. I'd missed it. What on earth would happen now?

I would take the exam on my own in the headmistress's office, that's what.

Looking back on it now, I believe that the diagnosis of glandular fever was wrong and instead it was stress, brought on by the impending exam.

My confidence in this misdiagnosis is inspired by what would follow in the years to come, beginning with my first year university exams.

I had passed the dreaded 11-Plus, navigated my way through GCSEs and A-levels, then went on to study business at the University of Sheffield.

If I was going to successfully follow dad into a managerial position, I was certain that a degree in business studies would be the path to get me there.

At the time, I had no bigger plans for my life than that.

Business studies.

Management.

Suit.

I found the first year of university relatively easy, especially compared to my Russian, maths and economics A-levels.

Easy that was, until exam time.

To revise for the first year exams, laden with textbooks, I returned home to the Wirral by train.

Mum greeted me at the station, taking me the remainder of the way home by car. During the journey, she said, "When we get home, ignore what dad says. He's saying some funny things at the moment."

I wasn't sure what she meant, but I remember being worried and confused by her words.

Up until this point, we hadn't been an emotionally demonstrative family. We didn't say, "I love you", or exchange much physical contact. It's fair to say that we were a stoic family.

If I was a little worried during the car journey, upon arriving home, I was petrified.

Looking like a shadow of the man I'd idolised all my life, dad fell into my arms.

Something was terribly wrong.

The man who always knew the answers to my questions; who could get us out of any jam, who could build a kitchen from half an ash tree and a boat from a fibreglass kit, was sobbing in my arms.

It was 1992, I was 19 years old and in a split second, my life had just pivoted.

The scene I'd witnessed as a three-year-old was replaying itself, but this time, rather than mum, it was me who was doing the cradling.

Bipolar disorder expresses itself in cycles and – having ridden a wave of highs for a number of years – dad was now experiencing a severe downturn and was in the grips of depression.

Things which before were easy and taken for granted, were now extraordinarily difficult for him.

Like getting out of bed in the morning.

Like showering and shaving.

Like getting dressed.

With my bedroom located next to the bathroom and my pillow positioned adjacent to the dividing wall between the two rooms, I heard dad cry the same words that I'd heard as a toddler, "I can't, I can't."

This became a daily routine. I would see mum struggle to get dad up, showered and shaved – tasks he would regularly abandon part way through and return to the psychological safety of his bed.

By the time I returned home to revise for my exams, mum had already taken a substantial amount of time off work to care for dad. With me now back for a few weeks, she rightly took the opportunity to return to work, knowing that dad wouldn't be home alone.

I wasn't at all prepared for how hard this would turn out to be.

At the dining room table, as I pored over my textbooks, dad stood over my shoulder, feigning interest in what I was studying.

For a family which didn't usually have much physical contact, almost hourly, dad would stand behind me and put his hand on my shoulder, craving human connection.

I didn't know how to behave or what to say, so I buried my head in my books.

This routine continued for a few weeks, until I returned to university.

In the days leading up to the exams, I began to feel exhausted; unable to concentrate upon my studies. It resembled how I'd felt in the run up to the 11-Plus exam. Surely I couldn't have glandular fever again, could I?

Sufficiently concerned about my deteriorating health, I decided to pay a visit to my personal tutor, who was also my lecturer for financial accounting.

When I arrived, the door to her office was already open, so I popped my head in to ask whether she had a moment to discuss how I was feeling. She said that she had a few minutes before heading to her next lecture, so in I went, leaving the door open behind me. It would only be a quick chat, I thought.

"How can I help?" she enquired.

"I'm exhausted," I replied.

"Not another one!" she said.

Clearly I wasn't the first student to report that they were struggling with their exam preparations.

"Is there anything in particular you're having difficulty with?" she asked.

Breathing more rapidly, my emotions began to rise. I struggled to get my words out. I didn't know what to say. How could I? I didn't even know what was happening.

On my first attempt, I got only part way through my sentence, "My dad's had a nervous...."

I could taste the salt of my tears as they rolled down my cheeks and into my mouth.

I tried again and, this time, just about managed to complete the sentence. "My dad's had a nervous breakdown," I cried.

She could see immediately that this was more than just exam stress and rushed to close the door, to give us some privacy.

I remember so clearly the act of her closing the door and I've come to understand why I paid such significance to it.

If she's closed the door, this must be serious.

I went on to describe in detail the events of the previous few weeks; how dad was like a different person and how it was taking a toll on me.

My story must have taken its toll on her too, as I saw tears well up in her eyes. I took this as another signal that my situation was serious, so now I felt scared. I had gone into her office hoping for a quick solution, like dad used to give me whenever I had a problem, but my childhood superhero was out of superpower. Instead, my personal tutor gave me a couple of options.

I could delay taking the exams until after the summer. There would be no shame in that, she said, given what I'd been through; or I could take them regardless and hope for the best. Either way, she suggested that I down tools immediately, not do any more revision and, instead, get some much needed rest.

I figured that going through the entire summer with the prospect of exams hanging over my head would make me feel even worse, so I told her that I'd go ahead and take the exams as planned, but do as she suggested and stop revising.

This felt really weird. I'd always taken my exams seriously and spent a lot of time revising for my GCSEs and A-levels. But here I was, with my first year university exams just around the corner. Instead of having my head buried in my books, I buried myself under the covers, got up late, watched movies in my dressing gown and went for gentle strolls through the Peak District.

Taking my cue from what I'd learnt at home, I kept my feelings to myself, choosing not to share my struggles with my housemates. It must have looked so strange to them, either like I was feeling super confident or that I didn't care.

In those days, you went in person to collect your exam results. Although I sat all of my exams that summer, I can recall collecting the result for only one of them, Financial Accounting.

As I approached my personal tutor nervously, she held out her hand with a folded piece of paper and said to me, "this is the most remarkable result I have ever seen." I unfolded the paper to discover that I had achieved a First.

By the time I returned home from university that summer, dad had worked in the water industry for 32 years, ever since he'd joined as an apprentice at 18.

Although he was still struggling badly with his depression, he wanted to try to progress back to work.

Dad and I met with his boss in the local pub, to talk through some potential options. He agreed that dad could try coming into the office one day a week, to see whether he could cope with a gentle introduction.

Even this proved too much so, aged just 50, dad retired through ill health.

Mum, however, was still working. Now that I was home for the summer, once again I picked up the baton to care for dad whilst she was at work.

One of the many things that depression steals from you is the art of conversation so, when I drove dad to his psychiatrist appointment, the journey was pretty quiet.

That was until he revealed, "you know, this reminds me of when I was 19, the same age as you are now."

"Really, how so?" I asked.

"I used to drive my dad – your grandad – to his appointments," he replied.

I was intrigued.

"Appointments for what?" I enquired.

"I used to drive him to have ECT," he said.

I'd never heard of it.

"ECT? What's that?" I asked.

I wouldn't have to wait long to find out.

Dad and I sat down in the psychiatrist's office and listened to him explain that, having already been prescribed a long list of antidepressants and mood stabilisers without success, dad was suffering from drug resistant depression. The only other option available to him was electroconvulsive therapy.

Later, dad told me that, in 1961, when he'd taken his own father for the same treatment, he would watch him receive an electric shock to his brain, without anaesthetic, in an attempt to relieve him of his depressive symptoms. Up to 15 mental health patients would be lined up at a time and, because there were no curtains between the beds, dad would be able to see each one, in turn, be shocked into an epileptic seizure. Not easy viewing for anyone, never mind a 19-year-old son.

Now, dad was being told he would need to undergo the same treatment he watched his father receive 30 years earlier. By 1992, although still described by some as 'barbaric', the procedure was at least somewhat more refined than it was when dad had watched his father get treatment. With apparently no alternative, dad agreed to a course of 12 treatments, two per week over the following six weeks.

In a private room, the anaesthetist administered a muscle relaxant, then a general anaesthetic, before a doctor placed electrodes to his two frontal lobes and administered an electric shock to his brain.

After four treatments, mum and I could see glimpses of dad's personality. Then, after four more, there was a noticeable improvement in his mood. After the final four treatments, we were delighted to have dad back to what appeared to be his normal self.

I too was feeling much better, so travelled back to Sheffield to begin my second year at university.

Now that dad was medically retired, 15 years before he had planned to finish work, he needed to create a new normal. Given the events of the past, it perhaps shouldn't have come as a surprise to me to learn, during a telephone conversation with mum, that dad's idea of a new normal involved selling the family home and moving 270 miles to the south coast of England.

As soon as they bought the house, dad once again employed his civil engineering skills and began plans to dramatically extend it. Stuart and I had both left home, so naturally he and mum were going to need a seven-bedroom detached house to themselves.

By the time I visited them for the Christmas holidays, planning permission for the large extension had been granted and dad was already wearing his hard hat.

Although this project was considerably larger and more complex than the previous one he'd undertaken, dad wasn't fazed one bit. Once again, I watched him whilst he was in his element, excavating the trenches with a mini digger, before a cement truck arrived to dispense the concrete into his newly-dug foundations.

Whilst dad was enjoying himself outside in the mud, mum was trying to retain a sense of normality inside the house. The distinction between the inside and the outside wasn't all that obvious, because dad had already removed the entire back of the house, leaving it exposed to the winter elements, except for a large polythene sheet.

In addition to having no back wall, there was no hot water for washing, or gas for cooking. But, just like when dad was ill, I heard no complaints from mum. Whilst dad worked tirelessly outside in the trenches, she battled on in the kitchen, heating saucepans of water for washing, then served up breakfast, lunch and dinner from a gas camping stove, whilst wearing a woolly hat and gloves.

By early summer, gloves were no longer required for cooking nor construction, as the building work neared its conclusion. After nine months of living in a state of chaos, things were finally beginning to settle down.

Or so I thought.

As the son of a lay preacher, during his youth, my grandfather was instructed to respect Sundays as a day of rest. This meant that he wasn't allowed to pick up even as much as a pair of scissors, since it would constitute work. I imagine that, for a young boy, this must have been excruciating. Perhaps it explains why he raised my dad with a completely different set of rules.

From a young age, instead of being told to down tools, dad was frequently told the polar opposite. "Don't be idle!" his father would yell at him, if there was even the slightest hint of him resting.

It obviously had the desired effect, since resting is something that I've rarely seen dad do, except when he sleeps. During one of his building projects, I vividly remember him taking a break from some construction work to eat dinner, only to fall asleep part way through putting a spoonful of strawberry ice cream into his mouth.

With the renovation on their new home now complete, driven on by his father's instruction, dad ensured that neither he nor mum would be idle for the remainder of the summer.

It was summer '93 and by now, stories of the gains that could be made in the buy-to-let property market had reached the *Daily Mail*. Over a bowl of Bran Flakes, dad concocted his next plan.

Chapter Two

WITH no time to waste before the start of the next academic year, in the space of a month, dad purchased not one, but four student houses. He deemed that none of the houses were fit for immediate occupation – even by student standards. Over the course of the summer, he and mum replaced four kitchens, four bathrooms and redecorated all four houses from top to bottom, with no outside help, all in time for the new student intake.

The summer's events suggested that dad's depression was now firmly behind him, as he appeared to be back firing on all cylinders. As was the supercharged Jaguar XKR that arrived on the driveway one early autumn morning.

With the student houses now complete, once again dad had time on his hands and he felt compelled to fill it.

I first learnt of dad's passion for cars in the late '80s, when I arrived home from school one day to find a Porsche 911 idling on the drive. Up until this point, he'd always owned 'regular' cars, a couple of Volvo 245s and Peugeot 205s; an Audi 80. Looking back on it now, I can see that something else may have been driving this radical, new purchasing behaviour. After all, the financial leap from Peugeot to Porsche was a significant one.

In cases of bipolar disorder, it's typical for sufferers to make large financial acquisitions when they are in an 'excited' neurological state and this has been true of dad over the years. The purchase of the Porsche typified this behaviour, as did the sudden desire to sell it, in 1992, as soon as his first depressive episode descended.

But by the autumn of 1993, dad was feeling buoyant and had cycled back to an acquisition phase. In the space of just a few months, he'd bought four houses, plus a high-end Jaguar.

Mum and dad now lived just 150 yards from the sea, which gave dad the perfect opportunity to reignite his other passion – boats. Up until now, his boat ownership had been limited to the yacht which we'd eventfully trailed down to Spain, plus a couple of small dinghies. With his appetite for acquisition now firmly in overdrive, dad's pursuit changed tack, from sailing boats to motor cruisers and with that, the swift arrival of a 32-foot Fairline.

With the new boat comfortably berthed in Lymington marina, dad turned his attention back to dry land. The student housing market was booming and with it grew dad's investment portfolio, from four, to five, then six, then seven houses.

Of course, all of them needed refurbishing to dad's high standards. So, as with the previous house purchases, he replaced each of the kitchens and bathrooms himself, whilst mum painted all three houses from top to bottom.

If all of this manual labour was taking its toll on his body and mind, we were yet to see it. Once the house renovations were complete, dad further demonstrated his passion for cars.

This time, instead of choosing the comfort of a luxury Jaguar, he opted for a bone rattling, 700 BHP, two-seater Caterham.

It didn't take long before the weight of all of this ownership took its toll. The first sign that there was a downturn in dad's mood was when he began to talk of selling his assets. Firstly, the newly acquired Caterham. Then, as his mental health began to spiral downwards, the Jaguar; then the boat. By the time he expressed his desire to sell all seven student houses, he was firmly back in the grips of severe depression.

When I graduated from university and returned home to begin my job search, dad was struggling badly, so mum and I adopted our familiar care routine. With me now home, she returned to work, as I took up the temporary role of looking after dad, whilst also scouring the 'Media and Jobs' section of *The Guardian* for a permanent position.

Dad was now under a new psychiatrist and, despite previously having been told that he was drug resistant, he was prescribed lithium in an attempt to stabilise his mood. In spite of the new medication, life was just like it'd been when he'd been ill in the past. Each morning, mum tried to coax dad out of the safety of his bed and into the bathroom to perform the impossible tasks of shaving and showering. From my bedroom, I heard him repeatedly sob those familiar words, "I can't, I can't."

Armed with a good university degree and an ambition for financial success, I set my sights firmly on a career in business.

Of my different university courses, marketing was the one which interested me the most so, when I saw a double page spread in *The Guardian* for the BT Sales and Marketing Graduate Training Programme, I was already salivating at the idea of fast tracking through the business into senior management. I sent off my CV in the post, complete with a carefully-worded covering letter.

A couple of weeks later, I was thrilled to receive an invitation to BT's two-day selection event in Milton Keynes. After successfully navigating the selection process, in the November of '95, I began the two-year training programme, launching my career in marketing.

Back home, dad's blackness was unaltered by the new chemical intervention, so his psychiatrist turned to the only treatment with a track record of helping him.

Just like in 1992, he was prescribed 12 treatments of electroconvulsive therapy. Once again, by the fourth treatment, his neurons fired sufficiently that he could see glimmers of hope; by the eighth his mood began to lift. Once he'd had the full 12 treatments, the dark clouds of depression had passed. Dad was back to something close to his normal self.

With recovery, came a familiar pattern. Whilst taking the mood stabilising drugs, dad felt suppressed; lacking in vitality. With his mood now improved, dad could see no benefit in taking them, only negative side effects. So he went cold turkey, without telling anyone.

With nothing to stabilise his highs, no sooner had he sold the remaining student house, dad was determined to reinstate his property portfolio. He immediately went on another recruitment drive, once again buying four student houses in quick succession, followed by several weeks of refurbishment. Four new kitchens, four new bathrooms and new paint followed.

By the time they'd finished the fourth house renovation, mum and dad were in need of a holiday, so I booked them a week away, in a small fishing village in Andaluçia. This region of Spain has one of the best climates in Europe, except, as they would discover, during the month of April. A week of rain left them short of things to do but, on one particular saunter down to the centre of the village, dad's attention was captured by the window of a local property agent.

Mum and dad departed from Spain without a suntan, but with two properties; a three-bedroom villa and a one-bedroom apartment.

Dad's plan was to keep the villa solely for the family to use as a holiday destination, whilst renting out the apartment to guests. However, in the few days whilst they were abroad, dad didn't have time to flesh out the small details, like how he would attract guests to the apartment. This was in the days well before Airbnb, so I was drafted in to employ my newly-acquired marketing knowledge, to generate sufficient income to cover the costs of the apartment.

I was in my mid twenties and fiercely ambitious. By now, I managed advertising campaigns at BT, during the days when we regularly reminded you that it was good to talk. This exposed me to lots of new experiences, including working with some of the best creative types in London, including film directors, copywriters and art directors. For a boy from an insular peninsula, these were thrilling times and I made the most of it, both inside and outside of work.

Living with three other BT marketing graduates, we had a whale of a time, always joking around, often having parties and sometimes drinking too much.

In addition to my day job, I managed the rentals for the apartment in Spain, dealing with guests, managing the upkeep and balancing the books. Dad's investments over the years had made me very comfortable in dealing with finances. His various financial exploits clearly had an influence on me since, during this period, I began day-trading shares. It was still the early days of the internet, but it was already possible to trade shares online, so I opened a share dealing account, then proceeded to buy shares in the morning and, if the market went with me, sold them in the late afternoon. I had a spreadsheet on my computer with all of my earnings, which showed that on some days I was making as much as £600. I had it all mapped out, projecting forward to the day when I could retire. 2002, I forecast, when I'd be the grand old age of 30.

What I hadn't factored into my calculations was the emotional toll dad's illness was having on me. Beyond the chat with my personal tutor at university, I hadn't sought out any support to help me cope with the debilitating experience of watching dad suffer so greatly. At the time, I didn't know any different and certainly didn't have the wisdom to know that you can't just plough on regardless during times of such emotional distress. But plough on I did, working at BT, managing the apartment as well as building my retirement fund.

Then, towards the end of 1999, things came to a head. I'd spent the previous six months planning and executing a very large tender for BT's main advertising contract. To the winning agency, it was worth many millions of pounds and it was my job to manage the tender process, so that BT got the right advertising agency at the right price. My boss, who had many years of experience running tenders like this, had recently left the company, so it was down to me to deliver the goods.

I thrived on the responsibility, getting immersed in judging brilliant creative work, negotiating the contract and meeting some exceptionally talented people in the process. Once the successful agency was appointed and the tender process was complete, I began delivering the advertising campaigns themselves. This meant working with internal stakeholders at BT, followed by crafting a creative brief for the agency, then working with them to produce the best possible advertising, whether that be for TV, radio or print.

It was a great job and I was lucky to be in such a privileged position, especially at such a young age. In the mornings, I bounded out of my house in Islington, then walked enthusiastically to the office at Holborn Circus, excited for the work that lay ahead. However, towards the end of November, the events of recent weeks, months and years began to catch up with me. I no longer had the energy to leap out of bed for work and everything, even simple things, began to feel more difficult. I felt scared.

The feelings were familiar, like prior to the 11-Plus and first year university exams. But I had a deeper fear. This is how dad said he felt when he was feeling depressed. Ever since dad had retired through ill health, I said to myself that there was no way I was going to let that happen to me. I wouldn't let work make me ill. I'd seen too much suffering, seen too many tears. I'd heard 'I can't' too many times.

In a state of fear and confusion, I resigned.

I arrived at work and asked to see my boss, the head of advertising. As soon as we sat down, I could feel myself welling up. Trying my best to hold back the tears, I went on to describe the pattern of the last few years, how dad had been terribly ill and that I was now finding things very difficult. I don't remember the exact words of her response, but they were along the lines of it being clear to her that I had things I needed to deal with and that she would accept my resignation.

And that was it. In 30 minutes, the job I'd performed for five years and competed against thousands of other applicants to secure, was gone.

In a twist of good fate, a very good friend of mine from university had just left his job at Sony, with the intention of doing some travelling. So in the evening following my resignation, I rang to ask him, "You know you're heading off to South Africa? Do you fancy some company?"

As soon as he said yes, I felt liberated and thrilled at the prospect of swapping my briefcase for a backpack. I immediately threw myself into preparations for what would turn out to be a four month trip. Feeling reenergised, I bounded into Covent Garden, first to STA Travel to arrange my flights, then to Cotswold Outdoor to source my travel gear. The process of buying the kit was an exploration in itself, choosing an appropriately-sized backpack, an effective mosquito net and a sleeping bag suitable for the South African climate.

Once I'd gritted my teeth through my final rabies vaccination, I was ready for my new adventure. So, instead of facing up to the reality of dad's ongoing illness and my unhealthy reaction to it, I boarded a train to Manchester airport, then a plane to Durban, leaving my problems behind me.

Chapter Three

BACK at home, there were no trains or planes, but there were more automobiles. Dad's portfolio was expanding. In quick succession, his garage saw the arrival of a 5 litre Mercedes, two Jaguars, then a TVR.

At the same time as his car collection was growing, the bungalow directly behind mum and dad's house came onto the market.

As a single storey dwelling, it was ripe for development. Dad was concerned that a builder would buy it and demolish it, then build a two storey house overlooking their back garden. He decided to thwart any such ideas by buying the property himself, then – rather like in the case of the Spanish properties – devised a plan.

Mum is a fabulous artist so, to support her vocation, dad decided to convert the bungalow into an art studio, where she could paint. Then, to generate some extra income, he thought that I could rent it out to artists who wanted a place by the sea where they could paint.

Once he'd finalised his plans, he set to work on site. It didn't take long for him to discover that the wooden frame building was rotten, so half of it would need demolishing and rebuilding. With the associated extra cost, dad scrapped his idea for an art studio and decided to rebuild the property as a bungalow for resale.

So for the third time in his life, dad hired a JCB – first to tear down the existing timber construction, then to dig the foundations for the new, brick building. By now he was approaching 60, but his age was no match for his determination, as he doggedly constructed the new dwelling.

By the time I returned from my travels, the work was nearing completion. Just like with his previous building projects, I was amazed to see how much he'd achieved on his own. But I was also concerned. I could detect that, now the work was coming to an end, his mood was beginning to turn and he was voicing worries about what he was going to do once the project was complete. I wondered whether the sound of the JCB had drowned out his father's childhood instruction, "don't be idle!" But now the project was finishing, in the relative silence he could once again hear his father's words.

His health deteriorated at an alarming rate and he was soon struggling to get out of bed, so mum and I finished off the final bits of decorating, before listing the bungalow for sale. I felt a sense of relief that together we could, at least, forget about the bungalow and concentrate once again on getting dad well.

This illusion was quickly shattered when the financial reality of the building work began to unravel. With dad unable to shower and shave, never mind examine financial records, I took it upon myself to analyse the monetary situation. With four student houses, two overseas properties, sports cars and a boat, the picture was complex. When I finished my analysis, I discovered that the total outstanding debt ran into six figures. I felt sick to my stomach. "How are we going to dig ourselves out of this mess?" I thought. Certainly not with a JCB.

After taking dad to see another psychiatrist, mum and I discussed how we might resolve the financial situation. Thankfully, the bungalow quickly attracted a buyer, partly easing the burden, but there was still an awful lot of money outstanding.

Even though previous psychiatrists had prescribed lithium with no success, dad was given another course, in the hope that it would stabilise him. Mum and I were accustomed to seeing drugs have no effect on his mood, so we weren't at all surprised to see him continue to suffer. It did, however, bring about a numbing effect on his emotions and he became detached from the financial situation, so mum and I continued our search for a viable solution.

As we did so, dad's health continued to deteriorate. Eventually, the doctor advised that he had little alternative than to turn, like other psychiatrists before him, to electroconvulsive therapy. Dad never liked the idea of having an electric current passed through his brain – who would? But, by this stage, he admitted that it was the only choice available. I longed for the treatments to pass, knowing that once he got to treatment number four, we could expect some hope; then, after another four, some improvement and after 12 treatments, I could look forward to seeing dad emerge from his blackness.

After six weeks, he had received the full course of treatment and was sufficiently engaged with the financial situation to suggest redeeming an endowment policy to clear the debt. It wasn't the perfect solution, since it had been taken out to clear the remainder of the mortgage on their primary residence, but it would at least clear the immediate problem. Once we'd agreed on this as our best available solution, dad cashed in the policy and soon received the resulting funds. I created a spreadsheet with a list of all the outstanding debts, then spent a full day online, repaying over £100,000.

With things beginning to settle down at home, I could direct my attention to restarting my career. The less-than-positive end to my experience at BT had left me doubting whether another role in marketing was the right choice. Perhaps even more impactful was my exposure to serious illness, which was now making me think that there must be more to life than working for a wealthy corporation, trying to make them even richer.

When I was working at BT, I'd received a call from our advertising agency, AMV BBDO, to enquire whether we had any spare rooms they could use, to conduct some work of a sensitive nature. I was intrigued. They explained that they needed to make some phone calls to the parents of children who had been killed in car accidents, to support the government's 'kill your speed' campaign. It really struck a chord with me and, whilst I was yet to encounter bereavement, through my experience with dad, I could empathise with the idea of how much those parents must have suffered from their loss.

When a role with the government's communication agency presented itself to me, I recalled this memory of its anti-speed campaign, making the decision to accept the job an easy one. I figured that employing my skills in a sector which could make a real difference to people's lives would add meaning to mine.

Using the skills I'd learnt at BT, I helped create advertising campaigns for clients including the Department of Health, the Royal Navy and the Department for Education. After a couple of years, the opportunity for a promotion arose, to become a client account director. Despite the interruption to my career at BT, I was still very ambitious, so it felt natural for me to apply for the new role. I was interviewed by my immediate boss, as well as another client account director and the HR director. As I left the interview, I thought I'd given a really good account of myself and that I had a great chance of securing promotion, which would place my career firmly back on track.

Later in the day, news filtered through that the interview panel had made its decision and was ready to share the result with me. I nervously headed back up to the interview room and sat down to hear the words I desperately wanted to hear,

"You have the job."

Or at least, that's what I thought I'd heard the HR director say. But as she continued, I realised that I was mistaken.

"You *had* the job. Until the last question, when we asked you what you'd do if you were chief executive. It's a bit of a trick question really, to check whether you're onside."

She went on to explain that, in my response to the question, I'd become so enthusiastic about what I'd do as the leader of the organisation that I'd pumped the table with my hand. She didn't like that. Nor did she like the way I had explained how I would try to improve the quality of our work, taking it as a criticism of her training programme. I was stunned. When they asked me whether I had any questions, I said that I'd better leave the room and get my thoughts together.

By the time a new role became available in a different department, digital communications, my frustration had abated sufficiently for me to secure the job. I already had digital experience from my days at BT and I had, of course, learnt how to build websites through dad's commercial interests.

◊

At home, dad had rebounded from his most recent depressive episode and was looking for new opportunities. He didn't have to look very far, because his next door neighbour had just demolished his house and was replacing it with five new apartments. The plot upon which mum and dad's house stood was identical in size, sparking dad's imagination.

Dad was abuzz with ideas, sketching out a variety of plans, until he settled on the concept of building five apartments and a bungalow on the current site, retaining one of the apartments for him and mum to live in.

With his broad idea established, he engaged the services of a local architect to flesh out the design. After a few iterations, he settled on plans which he was happy to submit to the local planning council.

After an eight-week consultation process, the council rejected the plans, so dad visited the planning officer to see how he could alter them, to satisfy its requirements. After lengthy discussions, he reengaged the architects, incorporating the council's feedback before submitting the revised plans for consideration.

Buoyed by the positive conversations with the planning officer, dad felt so confident that the new plans would be approved that, during the latest eight-week consultation process, he began searching for somewhere he and mum could live once their current house had been demolished.

It didn't take long for him to find and acquire a newly-built place in the nearby town of Lymington, where the boat was moored. The house was smaller than they were used to, but it would suffice until the latest construction project was complete, which he figured would last approximately a year.

When the house move and consultation process were complete, much to dad's surprise, the plans were again rejected. Given the amount of time and effort he'd spent incorporating the council's feedback, dad was far from impressed. In an attempt to make a breakthrough, he engaged a local planning consultant, whose experience he thought would tip the balance in his favour. After several weeks of meetings and several thousands of pounds in consultancy fees, dad was armed with sufficient new insight with which to rebrief the architects. They set about creating plans which dad hoped would finally satisfy the planning committee. He was ready for his next move.

Chapter Four

BACK in London, I was receiving a rapidly growing number of briefs from government departments, as they learnt of the excellent opportunity presented by the then, relatively new medium, of digital. When I'd first arrived in the new department, my boss and I split the client list down the middle. With the growing appetite for our digital services, my list had now grown to 36 clients. During one of my review meetings, I remember discussing the issue of my workload with my boss. He said that I needed to delegate more. "Who to?" I replied. He smirked in the knowledge that we were the only ones in the team with the experience to deliver the projects.

Over the course of the next few months, the workload was unrelenting. I was working long days, then returning home to manage the rentals on the Spanish property and spending a lot of time on the phone to dad, trying to help him with the housing development.

I began to feel a tightness in my chest, which I ignored, until tightness turned into pain. Experience told me that this wasn't a problem with my heart, it was stress. So, at the end of one particular day, I paid a visit to my HR director, the same one who'd turned me down for the promotion, to ask her advice on what she thought I should do. Once she'd listened to my health concerns, she said, "when I'm suffering from stress, I simply drink and smoke more."

Armed with her unhelpful advice, I informed my boss that I was taking two weeks off, not to drown myself in drink and tobacco, but sunshine.

I headed to Spain where, for five days I bathed under clear blue skies and restorative sunshine. Until, that was, I suffered my first ever panic attack. Having seen dad's illness follow him from one location to another, I'd observed that a change of scene was no guarantee of a change in experience. Now, sitting in our Spanish villa, I knew it first hand. As my chest tightened further, I felt like I couldn't breathe. I was petrified. I called my parents and as soon as dad picked up the phone, I broke down in tears. "I don't know what's happening to me," I cried. He said that he knew exactly how I felt.

With me still on the landline, he called an airline from his mobile phone, allowing me to hear him explain to them that he needed to get me on the first plane home.

I spent the remainder of my two-week holiday at mum and dad's house, where I began to think about my future. It felt like history was repeating itself. At BT, and now in my latest role, I'd become unwell as a result of stress. It scared me that this was how dad's career had ended. Was mine destined to go the same way?

Despite still feeling extremely vulnerable, I returned to work on the Monday morning and, as it turned out, prematurely. As soon as I got back to my desk, I felt completely overwhelmed, unable to face the quantity of unread emails in my inbox or the voicemails on my phone. I made a call to my parents and agreed to meet them that lunchtime, at Waterloo station. They suggested that I should visit my GP to explain how I was feeling. Dad reminded me that it was only a job and that my health was far more important. He also suggested that there might be another path for me, in helping him over the next year or so with the proposed housing development. Although at the time I was mentally too unwell to consider a change of career, his idea gave me some comfort.

Chapter Five

WHEN I visited my GP, as my tears began to flow, I explained that I was unsure whether or not I was suffering from depression. After taking me through a checklist of symptoms, of which I exhibited many, he suggested that my crying alone was a fair indication that I was depressed. His words scared me, for I knew all too well what this meant. Having observed dad's experience with medication, I declined the doctor's offer of a prescription for anti-depressants, but left the consultation with his note advising my employer that I needed some time off work to recover from my illness.

It took longer than I had expected; three months in total. I spent most of that time at my parent's house, being nourished by mum's home cooking. Towards the end of my convalescence, I revisited thoughts about my career path. I anticipated that if I went back to my existing role, I'd simply return to the same workload which had made me ill in the first place. I also remembered what dad had told me at Waterloo station: the idea of going into partnership and learning from him was very attractive and I'd always thought that, one day, I'd like to run my own business.

◊

In mid-2007, for the second time in my career, I resigned. Just like on the previous occasion, I immediately felt a weight lift off my shoulders, so wasted no time in getting to work.

If dad and I were going to realise our plans, we were going to need some finance, which meant that my university financial accounting course was about to come in handy. First, we called upon the expertise of dad's brother, Mike, who had spent 40 years working as a quantity surveyor, to help us estimate the build costs. Then, drawing upon his knowledge, I designed a huge spreadsheet, complete with macros and formulas, which calculated the cost of every item, from bricks to bathroom fittings.

Armed with my monstrously-sized spreadsheet, dad and I visited a commercial bank to ask for a development loan. We shared our plans and the breakdown of how much we wanted to borrow. They said that most people pitch to them with a few figures sketched on the back of a cigarette packet and that they were happy to provide us with an offer in principle for one million pounds.

Feeling full of confidence and pretty much back to full health, I was in my element. Working alongside dad to build something together felt like a dream. Health wise, he appeared to be doing well and I was learning from him every day. I wasn't missing my old life one bit.

With the building project imminent, dad thought that this would be a good time to rationalise the other areas of his portfolio, so he put the Spanish properties and the student houses up for sale. They were quickly snapped up by investors, so now it was possible for dad to realise his own dream. He'd always wanted to live on a boat, so the one which he had moored in Lymington marina was replaced by a much larger motor cruiser, a Princess 45, complete with comfortable accommodation, central heating and an entertainment system. It was certainly big enough to live on, at least for a while so, with mum in agreement, they sold their house and moved onto the boat full time.

With the finance for the development agreed in principle, we revisited the plans with the architects, made a few final tweaks, then submitted them for consideration by the council.

During this latest eight-week consultation process, I divided my time between working at my home, just north of London, and making regular trips down the M3 to visit mum and dad on the boat. With the winter weather and darker evenings drawing in, the challenges of living on the water became more apparent. Whilst the boat itself was warm and comfortable, its surroundings were beginning to turn less hospitable.

At night, the jetty upon which you approached the boat was poorly lit and was becoming icy. Whilst there were plenty of yachts and motor cruisers berthed in the marina, all of the other owners were sensibly tucked up at home, which created a feeling of isolation.

During the council's deliberation period, I could sense dad's levels of anxiety rising. Given the implications of their decision, it was understandable, but worried me nonetheless. If their decision went against us, I was concerned about the effect it would have on his mental health. After all, he'd invested a huge amount of time, effort and money into the plans, so it would be natural for him to suffer at least a little bit of a setback.

As the day of the decision approached, dad was becoming visibly more and more anxious. Just like when he'd been unwell in the past, the mornings were becoming more and more difficult. He was getting up later, finding it hard to shave and shower and voicing concerns about what might happen if the plans didn't go through. As a family, we decided that we would attend the planning committee's meeting in person, to learn our fate.

From the outset of the meeting, it was clear to us that, not only did the committee intend to reject this set of plans, but that they would have rejected any plans. They simply didn't want to see any development of any kind in the local area. I remember looking around the council chamber, observing one committee member asleep, as our future plans were firmly put to bed. As we left, dad said, "That's it then. It's over." I felt sick.

With all of his hopes pinned on getting the plans approved, within 24 hours of them being rejected, he became desperate. Through all of his previous cycles of depression, I'd never seen a deterioration in dad's mental state like this. This was different and it scared me.

Like most mornings when I'd stayed overnight on the boat, I was woken by the sound of the water lapping against the hull. However, on the day after our fateful meeting, I could also hear mum's raised voice from the cabin where she and dad slept. Concerned about what was going on inside, I opened the cabin door to see dad trying to smother his head with a pillow. The previous day, he'd said that it was all over and now it was clear to me that he had meant it. After grabbing the pillow, mum and I tried our best to calm him and reassure him that everything was going to be okay. It didn't feel like anything was going to be okay ever again, but I was prepared to say absolutely anything to stop him from harming himself. I felt panicked. We were on a boat in the middle of a marina, with nobody else around and dad was suicidal.

Mum and I agreed that he was too ill for us to manage by ourselves, especially on the boat. So, whilst I stayed with him in the cabin, mum left the boat to get a phone signal, then called the GP surgery to ask how we could get

him into hospital. She got through to a nurse who said that, whilst she could understand the position we were in, dad couldn't be admitted to hospital unless he'd made a more serious attempt on his life. There weren't enough beds.
It felt pretty darn serious to us, but despite our pleas, dad remained with us on the boat.

Whilst I'd seen dad ill many times before, this felt like a completely different level of gravity. Never before had it felt like a matter of life or death. This time it felt dangerous, like our lives were beginning to spiral out of control.

Chapter Six

UNTIL just recently, I'd been living my dream life, working with my dad on a project that I was passionate about and learning a host of new skills in the process. But now my world felt like it was unravelling. With dad so desperately ill, what was I going to do with my life? I didn't have the experience to continue with the project alone. We'd planned for this construction to be the first of many, with me learning skills along the way, so that I could project manage the next one myself. But now, I couldn't see how this would be possible. Instead, would I have to return to London for work? What would I do? Return to marketing? I had so many questions, but no answers. My head was spinning.

The following days and weeks were a real battle, with mum and I trying to keep dad's head above water. We knew that we had to get him back onto dry land so, dragging him around the local estate agents, we found a property that wasn't perfect but, given the circumstances, would have to do. With no property chain hampering proceedings, we were able to quickly complete the purchase and move in.

The psychological impact of dad's illness and the uncertainty about my future sparked a downward spiral in my own mental health. Becoming more and more afraid of being on my own, I spent less and less time at my own house and more time at my parents'. My world began to shrink.

I'd left my home, my friends and my job. I couldn't recognise my life and I felt like I was losing my identity. I continued to retreat, until the only place where I felt safe was under the covers. Poor mum, she now had her husband and her son under her roof, both of whom were suffering to the extent that they couldn't get out of bed.

Like a lot of people who suffer from depression, I found mornings the most difficult time of the day. Things which I'd normally do on automatic pilot now felt impossible; things like throwing back the duvet, placing my feet on the floor and getting out of bed. Instead, I'd regularly lay there for hours, trying to waste away the day until it was time to sleep once more. When you have depression, sleep is evasive, so lying in bed doesn't equate to sleep. But, regardless of whether I was conscious or not, my bed was where I felt safest.

In the battle against my darkness, the morning of 22 January 2008 began like any other. As had become the norm, by the time I'd managed to haul myself out of bed, mum was already downstairs in the kitchen, whilst dad was still in bed, trying to survive his own blackness. I managed to get myself into the shower, a major achievement, splash a bit of soap and water onto my body, then began to towel myself dry.

"What's that noise?" I thought to myself. I was sure that, despite having turned off the shower, I could hear running water. I checked the taps in the sink. No, they were turned off. Next, I checked the cistern. Nothing. So I got onto my hands and knees to check the toilet bowl itself. Still nothing.

With my towel wrapped around me, I opened the bathroom door to check the landing. But despite being no obvious sign of water, I could still hear a leak. There was only one room I hadn't checked.

I pushed open the door to mum and dad's bedroom, to discover that it wasn't water I could hear. It was blood. Laying motionless on his side, with his back turned towards the door, dad had both of his arms draped over the side of the bed. He was draining himself of life.

I leapt onto the bed, allowing me to see the source of the noise I had mistaken for a running tap. An already large puddle of blood was growing in the deep pile turquoise carpet. Straddling dad, I tried to stem the flow of blood by holding his severed arm vertically upright and screamed down to mum.

In the few seconds before she arrived, I discovered that not only was dad still alive, but he had one last fight left in him. Straining to pull his arm back down so that he could drain his remaining lifeblood, he begged me to let him die. No longer would he have to fight this monumental battle, day after bloody day.

Using all of my strength, I fought to keep his arm upright.

As soon as mum appeared at the bedroom door, dad's demeanour changed, as he sobbed to her, "I'm sorry, I'm sorry."

From where I was positioned, whilst I couldn't see it, I instinctively knew that it was there. I yelled out to mum, "Quick! Behind the door, the cord from the dressing gown!" Breathlessly, mum detached the cord and immediately handed it to me. As I tied it around dad's arm, I could see the tendons hanging out from his wrist, where he'd used a blade from a Stanley knife to cut through both of his arteries. With my adrenaline pumping like crazy, I instructed mum to call 999. Once she was connected, they talked her through what to do next, so she relayed the information to me. An ambulance was on its way.

My abiding memory from the immediate aftermath of dad's suicide attempt is of mum on her hands and knees, scouring the carpet and mattress, trying to scrub away the deep pools of blood. I returned to the bathroom, where the sequence of events had begun, but this time to wash dad's blood from my body.

That evening, when I visited him in hospital, I remembered what the nurse had told us when dad had tried to smother himself with a pillow. I wondered whether this subsequent attempt on his life was sufficiently serious to be considered worthy of a hospital stay. Dad was on the recovery ward, following reconstructive surgery on his wrist. His surgeon explained that the damage inflicted by the blade meant he'd had to tie up one of dad's arteries, but his hand would be okay served by just the remaining one.

By the time he was paid a visit by the resident psychiatrist, dad was sky high on morphine, so it wasn't surprising to hear him tell her that he felt fine, with no suicidal thoughts whatsoever. Although it was clear to mum and me that his new-found enthusiasm for life was down to the drugs, the psychiatrist didn't appear to factor this in and gave him the all clear to return home.

We were both left in disbelief at her decision so, along with my brother, who'd raced down from Sheffield, we went to see the doctor in charge. After explaining to him dad's history of mental illness, thankfully this doctor agreed that he should be taken to the local psychiatric hospital. Mum, Stuart and I breathed a collective sigh of relief.

As we had suspected, dad's medically-induced high was short lived. Once he arrived at the psychiatric hospital, he became extremely anxious and was put on suicide watch, with nurses checking on him every 15 minutes. He was also put on a cocktail of medication, some designed to nullify his psychotic thoughts and others to lift his mood.

Back at the house, as the reality of what had happened began to hit me, I entered the darkest period of my life. As my depression deepened, my appetite disappeared and I couldn't sleep. Whilst lying in bed at night, desperately trying to get some relief from my thoughts, I began to have flashbacks of what had happened, plus hallucinations of what appeared to be an old lady hovering above me. I was petrified.

Over the course of the next few weeks, this pattern continued; traumatic nights followed by hospital visits to see dad during the day. Whenever mum or I went to visit, we tried to encourage him into the lounge to sit with the other patients, in the hope that a break from the isolation of his bedroom would do him good. During one visit, I remember finding him in his favoured place, lying on the bed, but this time laying in the foetal position. As usual, I tried to coax him out of bed and into the lounge, but his state of mind was so fragile that he wouldn't even roll onto his back. Instead, he lay facing the wall with his eyes closed, wishing the day away until it was time to take his sleeping pills, to get a few hours' mental respite.

To get her own break from the intensity of the hospital, mum returned to her local art group, where a fateful meeting turned out to be a major turning point in our lives.

Valerie was new to both the area and the art group. Upon being introduced to mum, they quickly discovered that they both used to live in Godalming, Surrey, just 200 yards apart from each other. Then, Valerie explained that she and her husband, Andrew, were shortly moving into a house on Lentune Way in Lymington. In a strange twist of fate, it was 200 yards up the road from mum and dad's new house.

Unlike when somebody succumbs to a serious physical illness, such as cancer, in the case of mental illness, few people come running to support you. Rather, people tend to walk in the opposite direction. Not Valerie. As soon as she learnt what we'd been through, she was ever present, either visiting the house to check how we were all doing, or inviting us up to her place for a meal.

On one occasion, over a small portion of lasagne, Valerie casually asked me if I'd like to help her to paint one of the rooms in the local Baptist church. The idea filled me with anxiety. Ever since I'd been depressed, doing anything besides the very basics in life felt impossible. I didn't even have the strength to check my emails, terrified by what might be lurking in my inbox. Nor had I felt like returning any phone or text messages, not even to my closest friends. Depression was telling me that I was safest by isolating myself, away from any one or any thing.

This is how depression wins. It lies to you. It succeeds by feeding you thoughts which are the polar opposite of the truth.

You're not good enough.

You have no skills.

You have achieved nothing.

You'll never achieve anything.

You'll never be well.

You'll always walk alone.

Painting a church is impossible.

Somehow, though, through divine intervention or otherwise, I summoned the strength to accept her invitation and, in doing so, changed the trajectory of my illness.

As good an artist as Valerie was, she was rubbish at painting. Perhaps she did it on purpose, trying to help me by extending the project. Approximately four minutes into the undercoat, she abandoned her paint brush, gave out a huge sigh and said to me, "Oh this is ridiculous, it'll take us weeks. Let's go and get a coffee instead."

So over a flat white and slice of cake, Valerie and I discussed my experience of the last few months, dad's suicide attempt, how I was feeling and then, to faith. The latter part of the conversation didn't last long, because I didn't have one. Yes, I'd been to a Church of England school, but I hadn't practised my faith since leaving. She asked whether I'd like to join her at a service and buoyed by her genuine interest in my wellbeing, I agreed. That Sunday, I nervously stepped out from the safety of the house to join the congregation at Lymington Baptist Church. When I saw Valerie waiting for me outside, my racing heart rate dropped down to a more comfortable level. Upon entering, what first struck me was the warm feeling of community. Before the service began, I could see people of all ages hugging, laughing, chatting and sipping tea. I felt safe. From a place of total isolation, I now felt like I wasn't alone. Together we sang, we listened and as we departed, we embraced.

By the time we applied the final coat of paint to the church hall, my clothes and hands – as well as my hair – were all well covered in white emulsion. On the walk back to the house, I met a man walking his black Labrador. Intrigued by my appearance, he stopped to ask me what I'd been doing. When I explained that I'd been trying to get the majority of the paint on the walls of the church hall, he wasn't discouraged, so asked me, "Do you fancy a job painting a medieval house, down by the water?" He was a builder and needed another pair of hands, since the project was running behind schedule. So for the second time in a month, I said yes to a new experience and with that, I had a job.

Despite my new role, two events in quick succession demonstrated to me that I was still struggling. Not only does depression rob you of many mental faculties, but several physical ones too, including coordination. On my first day at the construction site, I was painting the wall of one of the upstairs bedrooms when I lost my balance, putting my foot clean through the newly plastered ceiling below. Thankfully, the other tradesmen gave me only the slightest ribbing, before repairing the hole I'd made, but my lack of coordination was a sure sign to me that I was yet to fully recover.

During my next visit to church, I received the second sign. With one service already under my belt, this time I felt more relaxed. However, it didn't take long for my calmness to turn into panic. Before the main service began, the pastor paid tribute to a young man in the congregation who the day before had taken his own life. I'd never met him, I'd never even heard his name before but, as the testimony continued, I could feel myself begin to tremble. As a rush of emotion swept over me, I became breathless. I couldn't sit any longer. Gasping for air, I ran out to the rear of the church. I wept, crying for the young man I didn't know and for dad, who I knew could so easily have experienced the same fate.

Needing to be on site for 7:30am proved to be a blessing in disguise. Whilst at first I found the early starts difficult, having a purpose gave me a springboard out of bed and into recovery. As well as my painting duties, I was put in charge of making cups of tea. On a building site, there isn't anything more welcoming than the sight of someone about to interrupt your manual labour with a hot brew, so I quickly made friends with the other labourers, giving me a much-needed sense of community.

The construction site was a long way from fancy advertising agency boardrooms, but I didn't care. I felt like I was doing something worthwhile. Through the new paint on the wall and the used cups in the sink, I could see the fruits of my labour at the end of each and every day. And I was recovering.

I was also making friends with the owners. With a complete refurbishment going on in one half of the house, Sean and Bella were raising their four children, including young twins, in the other half. As they grew to know and trust me, they asked me to help them with their chaotic schedule, so my duties were further extended, to collecting the twins from nursery. Feeling a new sense of community and with dad still resident in the local psychiatric hospital, I decided that my immediate future lay on the south coast, rather than in north London.

I put my house up for sale.

By now I felt detached from where I'd spent the previous decade. My career in marketing felt like a world away and dad's suicide attempt had moved his illness up another notch in severity, demonstrating to me that mum was going to need a lot of support to keep him out of danger.

There was also the treacherous issue of mum and dad's finances to resolve. They owned two houses, one of which now appeared to have very little hope of development, plus a very expensive boat moored in an equally expensive marina. Dad had been so confident that we'd receive planning permission on the third attempt that he'd begun to prepare the house for demolition. So gone were the carpets, light fittings, boiler and bathtub. Hardly the state in which to advertise it for sale.

As it turned out, we didn't need to. One day, out of the blue, I took a call from a man who said that he'd seen the house sitting empty and had asked our next door neighbour who owned it. He told me that he'd always wanted to live on that particular stretch of road and asked whether the house was for sale. I felt a surge of adrenaline; for the first time, I could see a way out of the dire situation which had led to dad's mental breakdown. Containing my excitement, I casually replied that I had no idea and would need to check with my parents. Little did he know that my dad was lying in the foetal position in a psychiatric hospital bed because of the house this gentleman wanted to buy.

At one nervy point in the process, it looked as though the house sale was going to fall through. The buyer called to say that the buyer of his own house had come back with a reduced offer so unless we reduced our asking price by the same amount, he would withdraw from the purchase completely. Unwitting to him, with dad desperately ill in hospital, we had little choice but to accept any offer at all.

We were clearly very lucky to find someone willing to buy the house with the state that it was in, but we weren't so lucky with finding a buyer for the boat. During the many months whilst dad lay in hospital, mum and I repeatedly visited the yacht brokers at the marina, hoping that they had found someone to alleviate us of this extra financial burden. On each occasion, we left disappointed. With every month that passed, its ownership was costing us significant berthing fees, so we decided to cut our losses, to the tune of fifty thousand pounds.

It was my desperate hope that, by removing dad's grave financial concerns, his state of mind would improve. But I was left disheartened when the positive news of the house and boat sale had no impact on his mental health. Despite another new cocktail of psychiatric drugs, dad's mood remained extremely black, so once again, the doctors turned to their treatment of last resort, electroconvulsive therapy.

After a course of 15 electric shocks to his brain, dad was able to leave psychiatric hospital. Upon his return home, whilst the treatment lifted him out of his depression, mum and I were concerned that it might have elevated his mood too far, such that he would begin another cycle of mania. When he and mum had first moved in, dad's illness had prevented him from doing what he'd routinely do after buying a house – assessing its potential for refurbishment. With his dark cloud of depression having cleared, he could now see a vision for the new space, so began to draw up some plans. Much to my and mum's relief, they were much more modest than his previous ambitions. Whether this was down to his age – he was now 66 – or his painful experience of the unsuccessful development, I wasn't sure. Either way, I was pleased to see that there were no plans for knocking down external walls or for large extensions.

Instead, they were limited to more common improvements, a new kitchen, bathroom and heating system.

Contrary to our earlier fears, dad's mood remained stable, allowing him to make good progress on the house and providing huge relief to mum and me. With our shared experience, we'd developed a very special bond. By now, it felt like we'd been fighting dad's illness and its fallout for a very long time. With the unpredictable nature of his illness, I still felt like I needed to be there for her, since neither of us knew how long this good spell would last. Mum, though, was equally concerned about me, "Perhaps it's time for you to get on with your own life. You can't put your life on hold for us forever," she said.

For a year, I'd been so concentrated upon mum and dad's plight that I hadn't given any thought to my own path. But I could see what she meant. I'd left my career, my circle of friends; I'd sold my house and moved back in with my parents. Hardly the trajectory I'd planned for my life.

Her poignant question coincided with me receiving an invitation to the wedding of a childhood friend, who lived on the Wirral. It'd been well over a decade since I was last there, so I was thrilled about the prospect of returning to the place I still called home.

I decided to make the occasion even more exciting by making the 270 mile journey by motorbike. Ever since I was a young boy, I'd loved motorcycles, but despite my passion, mum had always insisted that I couldn't have one – they were far too dangerous. More recent history had taught me that life itself could be dangerous and too short not to do the things you love. Soon after dad's suicide attempt, I passed my bike test and bought myself a brand new Triumph.

The beginning of my ride to the Wirral was an early indication that the journey north would be transformational. Only 20 minutes in, as I was riding along a straight stretch of road through the New Forest, I glanced to my left to see a deer running directly parallel to me. Through my elevated position on the bike, I could see over the hedgerow to watch it glide majestically across a field, at the same speed as me, as if we were riding in tandem.

As any motorcyclist will tell you, if you want to make the most of a ride, you're best sticking to A roads. With this in mind, I decided to avoid the faster, motorway route and instead take the long way round. From the New Forest, I made my way up to Salisbury, then on to Bath, before crossing the Severn bridge. After a thrilling few hours riding through the stunning landscape of South, then North Wales, I saw the landmark which told me I was just minutes from 'home'. Two Mills, the site of a former car dealership, sat on the intersection between the Welsh Road and Chester High Road. Although it'd been 15 years since I'd navigated these roads, I still knew every bump and turn. With a gentle flick of the bars, I glided through the familiar bends, past the rugby club, then my old grammar school. Old memories flooded back. Really good memories. Until this point, I hadn't realised just how much I'd missed this place.

After a soul nourishing two days of catching up with old friends, my mind was made up. Like mum had told me, it was time to get on with my own life, so I decided that I was going to leave the south of England to venture back home to the north west.

Although I was full of excitement at the prospect of moving, I knew that there was a chance that it could turn out to be the wrong decision. I was used to following my heart, but I was conscious that on this occasion I needed to use my head, so after the ride back from the wedding, I began my search for a flat to rent, in the knowledge that if worst came to the worst, I could easily reverse my decision.

Despite this knowledge, when it came to moving day, I was very emotional. After everything we'd been through together, leaving mum and dad was heart-wrenching. Whilst I was full of excitement for what lay ahead for me, I was worried about the situation I was leaving behind. As I hugged them both goodbye, my heart was full of emotion and my head full of concern. Would dad stay well? Could mum cope on her own? As I drove away in my heavily laden car, I looked into my rearview mirror and through teary eyes, I watched them disappear into the distance.

Chapter Seven

IT DIDN'T take long for my fears to be realised. I'd moved north in January 2010 and by the summer of the same year, dad was already beginning to struggle.

Following my move, I kept in regular contact with mum on the phone, so I knew that dad's mood had deteriorated. But, by the time we met for my brother's wedding in the August, I was shocked to see how bad he'd become. Having seen him ill so many times before, before he even spoke, I knew that his depression was back. All of his familiar symptoms were there: a scared look in his eyes, a grey complexion and very few words, except for "I can't." When we embraced, I could feel him tremble, a clear sign that his entire body was flooded with anxiety. Although I was best man, I was very conscious that he was going to need a lot of support just to get through the day so, added to my more traditional duties, was the role of chaperone.

I knew what was coming, so a week later, I wasn't at all surprised to receive a telephone call from mum to say that dad had been admitted to Winchester Hospital. What was surprising, was to learn that, despite his previous suicide attempt, getting a bed for him had been a real struggle. With dad's mental health record as poor as it was, mum had access to the mental health in the community team. When she began to fear for his safety, she called them to say that she needed urgent help. But because it was Friday evening, she was greeted with a message to say that there were no services until Monday morning. Dad's mental illness had no regard for what day it was, so mum called an ambulance.

By the time it arrived, dad was frantic, becoming irrational and refusing to get into the ambulance, so the paramedics had little choice but to leave without him. Mum immediately hid all of the kitchen knives, pills and anything else with which he could harm himself. After a sleepless night, she called a GP who she knew from church and he arranged for dad to be detained under Section 3 of the Mental Health Act. An ambulance soon arrived at the house, dad was sedated, then taken to hospital.

A new hospital and a new psychiatrist meant a new set of psychiatric medication, so dad spent the next few weeks under their influence, in a chemical fog. Just like on every previous occasion, the drugs didn't work, so once again, the doctors turned to the treatment of last resort. Twice a week, dad was taken from Winchester to Basingstoke hospital, to be administered yet another course of electroconvulsive therapy. After 12 sessions of ECT, dad was deemed sufficiently well to be discharged from Section 3 and return home.

Over the previous few years, mum had felt it necessary to sacrifice her own wellbeing in order to prioritise dad's, so on several occasions she postponed an operation to rectify a collapsed womb. By early 2011, the pain was becoming too much to bear so, as dad left hospital, mum was admitted for her own stay.

After the operation, mum required an extended period of convalescence so, whilst she recovered with friends in Guildford for a few weeks, dad came to stay with me on the Wirral. As soon as he arrived, I could see that, whilst the ECT had lifted his mood, he remained anxious. It was natural for him to be worried about mum – after all, other than his periods in hospital, they hadn't spent a day apart from each other in years. But this was more than worry. He was agitated to the extent that he couldn't sit for long, he had trouble concentrating and his sleep was beginning to suffer. When I suggested that we try to settle his mind by going out for a walk around the lake, he replied, "I can't," and then I knew. He was on the slippery slope towards another depressive episode.

From experience, I knew that once dad reached this point, his mental illness never went into remission without professional help. When I managed to secure an emergency appointment with my GP, she could see that he was fragile. In light of his history, she arranged for the mental health 'home team' to visit him each morning. It took only a handful of mornings before dad's state of mind deteriorated to the point where he couldn't get out of bed. When Neil, the gentle mental health nurse, asked him whether he could place a foot out of bed and onto the floor, dad insisted, "I can't." Whilst Neil didn't know dad well, like me, he knew the signs. He called the local hospital, Clatterbridge, to check whether there was a spare bed available in the psychiatric unit, Springview. We were in luck. Now we just needed to convince dad that this was the best place for him.

Thankfully, on this occasion, there was no need for sedation or a 'section', since dad agreed to be admitted. With both of my parents now convalescing, I visited dad at

Springview in the daytime, then in the evenings, phoned mum in Guildford to check on her condition. Whilst mum was making good progress from her own operation, dad's state of mind hadn't improved, in spite of another new cocktail of psychiatric medication. Just a few days after being admitted, he showed me some burn marks on his hand. I was shocked to learn that he'd put a metal coat hanger into a live electricity socket, in an attempt to electrocute himself. He didn't want me to tell the nurse. He said that if the hangers were taken away from him, it would remove the only means he had to stop his mental anguish. Fearing for his safety, I ran to fetch the doctor, who assessed his burns, then arranged for the nurse to swap the metal coat hangers with ones made from cardboard.

Two weeks after the incident, mum had recuperated sufficiently to leave Guildford, so drove up to join dad and I on the Wirral. Just like old times, we developed a tag team, with mum visiting dad just after his lunch, whilst I did the evening shift. After one of her visits, she returned to my flat admitting that she hadn't known whether or not she should tell me, for the fear of upsetting me... earlier that morning, dad had put a bag over his head to try to suffocate himself. I was more saddened for dad than upset for myself. It was another sign that his suffering had become so great that he had lost the will to battle his relentless illness. These two incidents made it clear to us that dad's hospital stay wasn't going to be a short one, so mum and I agreed that she should rent a nearby flat, where she could stay whilst dad remained an inpatient.

Dad persisted with his new psychiatric medication, whilst mum and I continued to visit him daily. After six weeks of taking the new cocktail, neither we nor the psychiatrist saw any improvement in dad's mood. Knowing that it had always helped in the past, he began another course of electroconvulsive therapy. This time, he needed only to make the short trip up in the lift to the ECT suite on the first floor of the hospital. After each treatment, we saw him return to his room in a slightly more elevated mood than when he'd left. Then, after six weeks and 12 treatments, he was well enough to be discharged, to join mum in their new rental property, just 100 yards from mine.

Up to this point, 30 years into his illness, dad had tried every conceivable type of medication; multiple anti-depressants, anti-anxiety pills, antipsychotics and mood stabilisers, none of which had any positive effect. As a result, upon discharge from Springview, the psychiatrist recommended that dad should have maintenance ECT every fortnight, in the hope that it would keep his depression at bay, at least enough to keep him out of hospital.

So, every two weeks, dad visited Springview as an outpatient, receiving a general anaesthetic, followed by an electric shock to his brain. For ten days after each treatment, occasionally a few days longer, he found relief from his depressive symptoms, but at a cost. His memory was wiped out by the regular shocks to his brain, especially his short term memory. Whilst he could recall memories from his distant past, he struggled to remember what he'd had to eat earlier the same day. But, with his medication proving ineffective and no alternative treatment to turn to, he had no real choice but to accept the significant side effects of having ECT every two weeks.

Attending hospital every fortnight, plus all of the regular blood tests and heart checks, meant that both mum and dad's lives had to be planned around his treatment, which forced them to remain relatively close to home. With their actual home 270 miles away in Hampshire, dad's new treatment protocol prompted them to rethink their long term plans.

With me living such a short distance from their rental flat, plus its proximity to the hospital, there were good reasons for them to follow in my footsteps by making their move back to the north west a permanent one.

After their minds were made up, I travelled down to Lymington for a week to paint the house from top to bottom, preparing it for sale. Following the refresh, I placed the house on the market with a local estate agent, then two days later received a call from them with an offer very close to the asking price. The sale went through without delay, meaning that mum and dad completed a move from the south to the north west, just like they'd done 35 years earlier.

For the year or so following my own move north, I'd been working as a freelance web designer and search engine marketer, utilising the skills I'd learnt during my career in London. But I still harboured ambitions to earn my fortune. One morning in March, I turned my dream into action by combining my skills in digital design with my passion for motorbikes, establishing an ecommerce business which sold motorcycle clothing and accessories. Whilst there were plenty of bricks and mortar shops in the UK selling motorbike gear, few had a good online presence. With my search engine marketing skills, I was confident that I could outrank them on Google, helping me to make my fortune. Marketing skills I had, but what I didn't have was any contacts in the motorcycle industry from whom I could source products. No problem, I thought, I'll simply get hold of a copy of the motorcycle trade magazine. In there, I spotted an advertisement for the forthcoming annual motorcycle trade show, which was being held at the NEC in just a few weeks' time.

Prior to the event, I registered my business with Companies House, then built a website to demonstrate to any potential suppliers that I was an established motorcycle retailer. I made sure that it looked the part, complete with products from the leading brands, absolutely none of which I sold. Or stocked. Or had even touched.

With my good friend, Mark, who was also a keen motorcyclist, I travelled down to the NEC, only to be met with disappointment. Speaking with the main distributors, I learnt that they weren't interested in working with online-only retailers. To do business with them, I needed to have a shop. One very large distributor proudly proclaimed to have turned down Amazon for the same reason. Unsurprisingly, they have since gone bust.

Just as my dreams looked as though they were going to be dashed, Mark spotted a small exhibition stand in one corner of the hall, showcasing some striking carbon fibre helmets. I learnt from the Polish salesman that they were hand made in Portugal, for a company which had been successfully selling in mainland Europe, but was now looking for retailers in the UK. He was interested to learn about my business, how long I'd been operating for, which brands I stocked and the size of my warehouse. "Does my bedroom count?" I wondered. To help convince him that I was a worthy business partner, I took out my laptop to show him my website. It worked a treat. To my delight, he said that he'd be happy for me to stock their helmets alongside the major brands I was already working with. After the paperwork was signed, I drove home with a big grin on my face. I had my first supplier.

After many years of working for large private and public organisations, I thoroughly enjoyed the fast pace and responsibility of growing my own small company. During the first couple of years, however, it wasn't as lucrative as working for someone else. I didn't pay myself for the first two years, instead investing the profits back into the business, whilst I lived off the proceeds from my house sale. Yet while running my own business didn't give me immediate financial reward, it did provide me with flexibility – not only to help care for dad, but also to do other things, like find my future wife.

Chapter Eight

IT WAS August 2012 and my beloved Liverpool were about to kick off their first home game of the season, against the Premier League champions, Manchester City. During the match build up, I picked up my phone to check the banter on Facebook. Scrolling through my feed, I was stopped abruptly in my tracks – not by anything football related, but by the sight of a beautiful woman. I didn't know her, but I did know the person in the photo standing next to her, a good friend and fellow marketing trainee from BT. Despite both of us having since left the company, we had stayed in touch. One of the things which bonded us was our mutual love for LFC. So, under the guise of the forthcoming match, I texted him to ask, "Who's the girl standing next to you in the photo on Facebook?"

After a pause, he replied, "What photo? What girl?"

"The one with the short hair," I replied.

"I don't know what you're talking about, let me check Facebook..." he said.

A couple of minutes later, after finding the photo in question, he replied, "Oh, that's my client, Pauline!"

Without hesitation I quipped, "Well, you'd better give me her number!"

Later that evening, out of the blue, I received an email from Paul.

To: Matt Janes   From: Paul Simon

Subject: Pauline

So then, she's happy to hear from you!

I told her what you said, that she looks 32.
She wants me to let you know that she's actually
46. (Do you still want her number, haha?)

Her email is [xxxxx@gmail.com]

Good luck... & god bless!

Paul

"He didn't actually ask her, did he?" I thought to myself, more than a little embarrassed. I wasn't used to randomly asking strangers for their contact details, but since he'd asked, and she'd said yes, I seized the moment.

The following morning, on the late summer bank holiday, I sent Pauline an email, with the subject line, "Thirty Two".

To: Pauline   From: Matt Janes

Subject: Thirty Two

Good Morning...

Mr Paul Simon is spreading rumours about your age, which I simply can't believe to be true. He even said you'd be happy to give me your email address, so the bank holiday must have gone to your young head...

Soon after, I received a reply, which led to another email, and another. We were getting on so well that we agreed to meet up for the weekend. So, two days after having been introduced, I booked the train to London and a two-night stay at the Strand Palace hotel.

Even on our first date, at the Lemon Tree pub in Covent Garden, we knew that we had a very special connection. Over a bottle of New Zealand Sauvignon Blanc, we discussed our respective backgrounds; where we'd grown up, our careers to date and, of course, our families. To describe the authentic story of my life, I needed to share my experience with dad's illness, not some glossy, Instagram version of it. As I spoke, it didn't take long for me to realise that Pauline could relate to the suffering. Once I'd finished my story, she spoke of hers. Of her upbringing in Toronto. Of her parents, who were born in Slovenia, but who had emigrated to Canada in the 1950s to find work. And of Michael, her late husband.

Pauline shared how she and Michael had already been together for 17 years when they got married, in Princess Margaret hospital, Toronto, six weeks before he lost his life to cancer. It was rare for me to meet someone who could empathise with the pain of seeing a loved one suffer from a chronic illness. Pauline was different – she had cared for Michael for five years, whilst he had battled leukaemia.

Following Michael's premature death, Pauline remained in Toronto for a couple of years, before moving to Vancouver, to work on the 2010 Winter Olympics with Royal Bank of Canada. It was there that she grew her reputation for expertly managing large-scale hospitality events. As a result, when Lloyds Banking Group was looking for someone to lead its hospitality programme for the 2012 Olympic Games, it turned to her expertise, relocating her 4,500 miles to London.

The Olympic closing ceremony had taken place three weeks before we met and I was excited to learn that she intended to stay in London, rather than return to Canada. Our relationship blossomed, so we spent alternate weekends travelling between Swiss Cottage and the Wirral. Lured by the natural beauty of the peninsula and walks along the beach, a year later, Pauline relocated from London, moving in with me and my Doberman, Indiana Janes.

Meanwhile, whilst dad was doing well on his regular schedule of electroconvulsive therapy, his memory had become so poor that he'd decided to try reducing the frequency; every three weeks instead of every two. With the reduced treatment, it took only six weeks before his mental health deteriorated to the point where, for his own safety, he needed to be admitted into hospital, which meant another stay on the ward at Springview.

Although I'd told Pauline about dad's illness, up until this point, she hadn't witnessed it first hand. Through Michael's illness, she was very accustomed to hospitals, but she wasn't prepared for what she saw during dad's admission to Clatterbridge. On arrival at the hospital, dad was assigned a large, yet sparse room at the end of the corridor, fitted out with just a bed, desk and a wardrobe. As Pauline grabbed dad's bag of clothes and proceeded towards the wardrobe, it was clear to me that she wasn't fazed by the hospital surroundings. However, when she opened the door to hang dad's clothes, her demeanour changed.

When she saw that the coat hangers were made from cardboard, rather than metal, wood or plastic, it dawned on her that suicide was a very real danger here. I could see that she was visibly shaken, so I walked towards her, comforting her with one hand and with the other, removed the cord from dad's dressing gown. What had once helped me to save his life now represented a threat to it. Surreptitiously, I slipped it into my jacket pocket.

Pauline was soon familiar with the hospital routine that mum and I were already so used to. A prescription for a new mix of psychiatric medications, which had no effect on dad's state of mind, followed by the psychiatrist's recommendation for dad to have electroconvulsive therapy twice a week.

After a couple of weeks of treatment, he was considered well enough to be reunited with mum in the flat, whilst continuing the course of ECT as an outpatient. To begin with, he was treated twice a week, then, as his mood lifted, once a week. When his mood stabilised, he returned to his maintenance dose of treatment every two weeks. Given the experience of the previous few months, it was obvious to everyone that, to keep dad out of danger, he was going to require treatment every fortnight on an ongoing basis.

During this schedule, we saw a regular pattern in his mood. For between ten and 12 days following ECT, he had relief from his depression, after which his mood rapidly deteriorated, until it was restored a few days later by his next treatment. It was a punishing schedule that continued for two years, until he began to voice concerns about being given a general anaesthetic and electric shock every two weeks. He said that he was scared that he would die on the treatment table.

It was an impossible dilemma. We knew from experience that if he didn't have ECT, he would become extremely ill, most likely resulting in another hospital admission. Equally, we couldn't ignore his concerns. ECT is considered a safe procedure, but by this time, dad had been given a general anaesthetic every two weeks for several years which, at 74 years old, was clearly worrying him.

After a great deal of contemplation and discussion, both within our family and with dad's mental health support team from Clatterbridge, we decided that it was only fair to let dad have the final say.

He made his decision, he didn't want any more treatment, he'd had enough. So in spring 2016, for the first time in many years, dad stopped having ECT, leaving only his antidepressants to support him.

Three weeks after he stopped treatment, dad became a danger to himself. Whilst mum called the crisis team, I did a sweep of the flat, removing kitchen knives, pills and any other items which could pose a threat to his safety. Later the same day, and for the sixth time in his life, dad was admitted to psychiatric hospital.

After all the years of visiting dad on different psychiatric wards, I had become accustomed to seeing all kinds of patients, young and old, men and women, in different states of mental despair. Years earlier, I had made a rule for myself that I would make a point of saying hello to every patient I encountered, regardless of their mental state. Some looked like ghosts, standing dead still in the corridor, whilst others were frantic, screaming in despair, but whatever their condition, I was determined to acknowledge their humanity by greeting them.

To this day, two particular patients stick in my mind. David, an 80 year old gentleman who, convinced that he was John Lennon, gave me a full rendition of *Imagine*. Then, a young woman, maybe 18 or 19 years old, who was experiencing psychosis. During one visit to see dad, after I hugged him goodbye, she came over to whisper in my ear, could she too have a hug? She craved human connection so, as I gave her a warm embrace, I felt her clinging onto me for dear life.

Something that was consistent, regardless of which hospital dad resided in, or which psychiatrist treated him, was the approach. By the time of dad's sixth admission, he'd been prescribed dozens of different psychiatric medications, none of which had ever helped him get well. Despite this fact, as soon as he was admitted, his medication was reviewed, then changed to a new cocktail. Unsurprisingly, it failed to have any impact, so the psychiatrist suggested more ECT. With his mental health having deteriorated so badly since he'd raised concerns about dying on the treatment table, dad gave his consent to yet more general anaesthetics and electric shocks. Anything to get some relief.

Michael had received such tremendous care during his battle against cancer that, after he died, Pauline decided that one day she'd like to give something back. After moving from Canada to the UK, she learnt of a charity called Maggie's, which specialises in cancer support, delivered through 20 centres around the UK. As destiny would have it, Pauline discovered that there was a centre just up the road from where we lived, Maggie's Merseyside. Remarkably, it was situated just two hundred yards from Springview, where dad was staying.

By the time that dad was admitted for his latest stay, Pauline had already been volunteering at Maggie's for a year, supporting visitors and their families, as well as helping to raise funds for the charity. On Friday mornings, en route to Maggie's, Pauline and I would sometimes stop at a café for breakfast. On one particular Friday, over a bacon sandwich, my life began a radical transformation, which we now refer to as 'The Bacon Sandwich Moment'.

Chapter Nine

BY THE time of The Bacon Sandwich Moment, I'd been running my business for five years. Since I ran the entire operation on my own, during this five year period, the only holidays I'd taken were two long weekend breaks. As a result, I was physically drained, which, when combined with the emotional toll of dad's illness, left me exhausted. A week earlier, I'd visited my GP to tell her I'd been experiencing chest pains. Looking concerned, she placed a stethoscope on my chest, only to inform me that whilst my heart sounded fine, I wasn't breathing properly. She said that I was suffering the ill effects of prolonged stress.

When Pauline and I sat down to eat our bacon sandwiches, I blurted out to her, "That's it. I can't do this anymore!"

I could tell immediately by the look on her face that she was scared. "Can't do what?" she asked timidly, fearing what I was about to say.

Despite having spent the last five years growing the business, I told Pauline that I was going to sacrifice it, for the sake of my wellbeing. It was a lot to take in, but after I explained how I'd been feeling, she responded by saying that I must do whatever I needed to do to restore my health. If that meant ditching the business, then so be it. Forget the money, forget the years of investment, just get well. She'd already lost one partner to illness, she wasn't going to lose another.

That same day, I began the process of clearing stock from the office, which I rented from another business operating from the same building. As I carried some stock along the corridor, I bumped into a couple of guys from the other company, who asked what I was doing. When I explained that I was closing the company, they quickly pricked up their ears. What began as a casual chat in a corridor ended as formal negotiations, so over the course of the next few weeks, we met several times to agree a deal for them to buy the business.

Whilst the proceeds from the sale may not have been sufficient to satisfy the fierce ambitions of my younger self, they were enough for me to take some time out, firstly to regain my health, then to take stock of my life.

Having worked for 20 years since graduating from university, I was approximately halfway through my working life. During which time, I'd worked a wide variety of jobs: in marketing for a large corporation, as well as central government; I'd worked as a labourer and run my own business. But despite all of these different roles, I knew that there was something missing, I hadn't found what the Japanese call their 'ikigai'.

By chance, less than two weeks after The Bacon Sandwich Moment, my friend Matt called, offering me the opportunity to join Providence, an executive coaching programme run by his company, Form. Matt explained that the programme included a number of one-to-one sessions with a mentor, as well as 'a two-day residential retreat in an inspirational venue, to unwind, reflect and make brave choices about your future.'

As the second half of my life lay ahead of me, I certainly had brave choices to make. In the quest to discover my own ikigai, I signed up for the six-month programme.

I first met my mentor, Mark, in The London Carriage Works, a restaurant in Liverpool's Georgian Quarter. Arriving on my motorbike, I took off my helmet, greeted Mark, then sat down with a mixture of nervousness and excitement.

"So then, Matt", Mark began. "Would you like Providence 'lite', or the complete, 'pull the drains up' version?"

I knew that if I was going to finally answer the call, to identify my true purpose in life, I was going to have to do some deep, deep, inner work. So without hesitation, I replied, "Let's pull the drains up."

Over the course of the next three hours, Mark asked me to share every aspect of my life with him, including my upbringing, my relationship with Pauline, my career, my hopes and my dreams. We spent a long time discussing dad's illness, including how it had affected my view of the world. After I described what it had been like to support him over the previous three decades, Mark said that he wasn't at all surprised, given everything I'd been through in my family life, that I'd found it hard to find a career which felt worthwhile. He also told me that the forthcoming retreat in Anglesey would provide me with the time, space and nourishment I needed, to discover who I really was and what I wanted from my life.

So in a comfortable Welsh cottage in the middle of nowhere, I spent two days with seven other delegates, most of whom were also at a crossroads, searching for something more meaningful in their lives. Together, we listened, we learnt, we talked and sometimes, we cried.

When I arrived home, I reviewed the notes I'd made during the retreat. Amongst them were two sentences which leapt out at me,

To find your true purpose, you need to dig into the pain and uncover the truth.

And

To write your story, listen to your heart.

I was pretty sure that, up until this midpoint in my life, none of the career advice I'd been given involved using my pain and my heart as navigation tools. Instead, my head and my wallet had always been firmly in the driving seat. Whilst this approach had led me on the path to managerial jobs and commercial success, it left me feeling empty and ill. Perhaps it was time for me to use a different compass.

When Mark and I had met for our first coaching session, he had been very direct in enquiring about my relationship with Pauline.

"Is she a keeper?" he asked.

"Yes. Definitely," I replied.

There was no doubt in my mind.

Just a couple of weeks later, during a discussion about my future path in life, Pauline casually asked me whether I ever wanted to get married. "Yes!" I replied immediately, then in unison, we said, "What just happened?"

Whilst Pauline hadn't directly asked for my hand in marriage, we were both very excited at the prospect of spending the rest of our lives together. I shared with her the news that during my recent deliberations, I'd been giving a lot of thought to our relationship and had intended to ask her to marry me on our forthcoming trip to London. So, on a beautiful spring day, in the tranquil surroundings of Kensington Palace Gardens, Pauline and I got engaged.

Whilst we were there, I recounted the story of what dad had told me during my fruitless years of dating, "The trouble with you, Matt, is that you're looking for someone as good as your mum. I'm sorry to tell you, but you're not going to find her."

He was almost right. It'd taken me 40 years.

Whilst my personal life was mapping out, I was finding it more difficult to identify the path for my professional life so, a couple of weeks after we were engaged, we headed to southern Spain, allowing me to deepen my contemplation.

There, whilst lying in the restorative sunshine, I read a book written by a neurosurgeon, called *Into the Magic Shop*. Whilst I read, I made some notes alongside those I'd made during my coaching session, jotting down the words which spoke to me the most, hoping that they'd provide me with some inspiration. When I reviewed them, I noticed a pattern.

A wounded heart – the biggest opportunity
for growth.

Ignore your heart and it will eventually make
itself heard.

They sat opposite the words which had resonated with me so much following my session with Mark:

To write your story, listen to your heart.

To find your true purpose, you need to dig into the pain and uncover the truth.

After all the years of being directed by my head, when I looked within my heart, like the sea that lay before me, my true purpose in life became crystal clear. I finally knew what I was here for.

Saving dad.

As this new vision for my life emerged, I couldn't help but be drawn by how my notes ended:

Now create your own magic.
Teach others.
Make it extraordinary.
Use your heart and your brain together.

I kept rereading that last sentence, 'Use your heart and your brain together.'

Chapter Ten

I HAD another epiphany. If I was going to use my heart as a compass, to learn how to save dad, I needed to fully understand the brain.

Instead of returning from Spain wishing that I was still lying on the beach, I arrived home with a huge sense of anticipation. As soon as we'd unpacked our bags, I opened the laptop and typed into Google, 'best neuroscience courses'.

Within the top search results was a course which immediately caught my eye. Clicking on the link, I read the course description:

"An intensive introduction to topics in neuroscience, ranging from the inner workings of neurons, to the function of small neuronal networks, to the function of brain systems that give rise to perception, thought, emotion, cognition and action."

It sounded perfect. There was only one problem. Harvard University was 3,000 miles away.

As I dug deeper into their website, much to my delight, I discovered that they offered the same course online as they did on campus, complete with exams and certification. So without hesitation, I entered my payment details to enrol.

The neuroscience course set off within me an insatiable appetite for learning. Once I'd mastered action potentials, voltage-gated ion channels and long-term potentiation, over the next two years, I took course after course, in the quest to understand how to get dad well, gaining certificates in the following:

Psychology and Mental Health
(University of Liverpool)

Foundations of Functional Medicine
(Institute for Functional Medicine)

Clinical Solutions for Addressing the Underlying Causes of Disease
(Institute for Functional Medicine)

Foundations of Heart Rate Variability
(Elite HRV)

The Power of Awareness
(Greater Good Science Center)

With my areas of study aligned to my purpose, textbook after textbook, everything sank straight in. However, I knew that as the volume of information grew, I was going to need a system for cataloguing my newly acquired knowledge. Utilising my digital skills, I created an online library, making it easy for me to search for and find everything I'd learnt, which proved invaluable in what was to come.

On my journey towards understanding dad's illness, I learnt that there was much more to mental health than just brain health. However, it struck me how, for the 400 years since Descartes had proclaimed, "I think, therefore I am," and despite a clear brain-body connection, dad's mental illness had always treated in a disembodied manner, as if his brain was detached from his body.

As I reviewed what I'd learnt so far, the words which had started me on this path echoed in my mind,

Now create your own magic.
Teach others.
Make it extraordinary.

Whilst I didn't have the key to unlock dad's suffering, I knew that I'd learnt enough magic to help at least a few people living with the same illness. Combining the knowledge I'd gained from my various courses, I wrote a 25,000 word manuscript, before filming, editing, then publishing an online course called Thrive, to help people better cope with stress, anxiety and depression. I was doing what the book had taught me, teaching others.

During the recent years of study, my income had been limited to what I'd earned from some small scale digital marketing, which wasn't very much. When it came to launching Thrive, I felt torn between charging for the years of investment I'd put into it, versus potentially preventing people from being able to take the course due to affordability. The decision weighed heavily on my mind, so I turned to Mark, my mentor, as well as other friends, for their advice. They all confirmed what my heart was telling me.

With Thrive now freely available online, I refocused all of my attention on how I could save dad from his depression. It'd now been over four decades since I'd seen him crying in the kitchen, so I was desperate to find something to end his years of suffering. I reviewed my notes, to discover a list I'd made of the medication he'd been prescribed. It wasn't exhaustive, just the ones I could remember, but still amounted to quite a collection:

Quetiapine

Escitalopram

Mirtazapine

Lamotrigine

Depakote

Fluoxetine

Diazepam

Propranolol

Venlafaxine

Lithium

Citalopram

Pregabalin

Aripiprazole

Amitriptyline

In addition to the drugs, he'd been treated several hundred times with electroconvulsive therapy, which he was still being administered every two weeks. This worried mum and me. We knew the devastating toll it'd taken on his memory, but what we didn't know was how it would affect his brain longer term.

Now 75, it was natural that he was slowing down, so it was no surprise to us when he developed soreness in his knee, creating a slight limp on his right side. Mum arranged for him to see Sue, a friend and experienced physiotherapist, who worked just up the road from where they lived. Upon assessing him, Sue found that there was a lack of mobility down the right side of his body, including his hand and facial muscles, telling us that it was worth further investigation.

Due to the fact that he was receiving ECT as an outpatient, dad had regular visits at home from the community mental health team so, during their next visit, we told the nurse of Sue's advice. The nurse agreed to report it to dad's psychiatrist, who arranged for him to see a neurologist.

A month later, mum and I took dad for his consultation. After performing a thorough examination, the neurologist informed us that, whilst he would need to arrange a brain scan to confirm his diagnosis, he believed that dad had Parkinson's disease.

During the appointment that followed dad's brain scan, the neurologist showed us an MRI of dad's brain. From my studies in neuroscience, I could immediately identify an area of the brain called the substantia nigra, which produces the neurotransmitter, dopamine. The image showed that dad's left substantia nigra was producing significantly less dopamine than his right, which explained why the mobility on his right side was becoming limited (the left hemisphere of the brain controls the right side of the body).

So it was confirmed, as well as major depressive disorder, dad was suffering from Parkinson's disease. His new diagnosis meant that his antidepressant medication was now supplemented by L-DOPA, a drug designed to help his mobility. When I asked the neurologist about the role that electroconvulsive therapy might have played in the development of dad's Parkinson's, he said that there was no evidence linking the two and that having the disease wouldn't prevent dad from continuing with ECT. As we left the neurologist's consultation room, mum and I exchanged looks, acknowledging to each other that our battle had just become even bigger.

News of dad's diagnosis was a big blow. I was worried about the impact it would have on his physical health, but equally as concerned about how it would affect his mental health, in the knowledge that Parkinson's disease often exacerbated depression, due to the role that dopamine plays in regulating mood. Driven on by this added anxiety, I extended my research to YouTube.

There, I discovered a doctor from the US called Dr. Kelly Brogan, who was being interviewed on the Joe Rogan show. Over the course of the three-hour interview, I found myself nodding in agreement with a lot of what she had to say about mental illness and the role that psychiatry played in treating it. It was refreshing to hear such a highly-qualified psychiatrist challenge the status quo, suggesting that there might be another path to vitality.

During the interview, she made fleeting reference to another doctor, Dr. Nicholas Gonzalez, whose wisdom, she said, had transformed her understanding of how to treat disease. Feeling inspired, I went online to research his work, where I discovered that he had achieved extraordinary results in treating cancer patients, yet despite his remarkable outcomes, he was disregarded by many traditional oncologists as a quack. I was intrigued.

Whilst neither my family nor I had ever been touched by cancer, Pauline's experience of losing Michael to leukaemia gave me a voracious appetite to learn more about this deadly disease, as well as Gonzalez's work. Down the rabbit hole I went, buying text book after text book, becoming utterly fascinated by the knowledge contained within.

I discovered that Gonzalez had developed a unique protocol for treating cancer, which built on the research of other exceptional doctors who had come before him. So, after I'd finished reading about his work, I read multiple research papers written by Dr. John Beard, Dr. Francis Pottenger, Dr. Weston Price and Dr. William Kelley.

After months of investigation, I now understood not only the fine details of his treatment protocol, but also the biology of how it worked. I learnt that there were three separate elements to the Gonzalez protocol; pancreatic enzymes, body detoxification and a personalised diet according to something he referred to as the patients' 'autonomic type.'

He was describing the autonomic nervous system, something I'd learnt about during a number of my courses. I knew that this part of the nervous system, over which we have no conscious control, played a role in disease, but it wasn't until I read Gonzalez's book, *Nutrition and the Autonomic Nervous System*, did I appreciate to what extent.

Towards the end of the book, he described the work of Dr. Daniel Funkenstein, a professor of psychology at Harvard Medical School, who researched the link between the autonomic nervous system and mental illness.

Gonzalez was adamant that if Funkenstein's work had been taken more seriously, it would have changed the course of psychiatry forever. I was bowled over.

There hadn't been a new treatment for depression in over half a century and here was a doctor saying that the industry had missed the opportunity for a revolution. He went on to say that, although Funkenstein's research was never widely adopted, it had been taken very seriously by another doctor, Dr. Ernst Gellhorn, during the 1940s, '50s and '60s.

I wondered whether there was something hidden in the work of these two doctors that could offer hope to dad, as well as other sufferers, so I searched for three specific textbooks to add to my collection.

Mastery of Stress
by Dr. Daniel H. Funkenstein (1957)

Emotions and Emotional Disorders
by Dr. Ernst Gellhorn (1957)

Autonomic Imbalance and the Hypothalamus
by Dr. Ernst Gellhorn (1963)

They'd all gone out of print many years earlier, so I scoured eBay and Amazon for second hand copies. Then, I discovered a possible reason for why they hadn't been read more widely. The price. Some cost over £300. It was a risk but, given what they could potentially teach me, one I thought was worth taking.

As soon as they arrived in the post, I jumped straight in, underlining all of the most pertinent points. I learnt the intricacies of the autonomic nervous system, including that it was controlled by part of the brain familiar to me from my Harvard studies, the hypothalamus. It was all finally beginning to make sense.

I learnt that everyone has a genetically determined and different physiology, biochemistry, psychology and health profile, which is orchestrated by the autonomic nervous system. My fascination deepened further when I read the chapters on ECT, the treatment which dad was still so reliant upon. I learnt why it worked for some people, like dad, and not for others.

Then came a light bulb moment.

During his time working in hospitals, Gellhorn discovered that his psychiatric patients had a dysregulated autonomic nervous system. The autonomic system is just that – autonomous. It's a series of muscles, organs and nerves over which we have no conscious control and it's now well established that the autonomic nervous system needs to be in balance for us to maintain physical health. What I had just learnt from Gellhorn was that the same is true of mental health.

My heart raced. Had I just discovered the origins of mental illness?

Crucially, when his patients were ill, this system was out of balance. But when they had recovered from their mental illness, autonomic balance was restored.

For somebody suffering with depression, mornings are often the most difficult time of day. One particular day of dad's, just a week before Christmas 2018, began especially badly. In addition to the routine chemical fog from his psychiatric medication, he awoke with pains in his chest. Concerned that all of the electroconvulsive therapy he'd received might now be affecting his heart, he told mum that perhaps they should call the doctor. Mum phoned the surgery, who, after checking dad's extensive medical file, told them to come in immediately.

After performing some checks, the doctor told dad that he needed to go straight to A&E, where he was taken by ambulance. He spent the day being given a variety of tests, which indicated that his heart was functioning within its normal limits.

However, on the second Tuesday in January, when they arrived at hospital for his ECT, mum and dad were informed by the anaesthetist that he wasn't prepared to administer the treatment until further investigations were made. He explained that he was concerned that both the anaesthetic and the electric shock could pose a risk to dad's heart.

When mum called me to explain that dad was unable to have treatment, I was extremely worried about his mental health. Personal experience told me how this was likely to end.

Sure enough, three weeks later, dad's mood began to dip, then, within another ten days, his depression had become so bad that we had to call the crisis team at Clatterbridge hospital. By now, they were very familiar with dad's history, so when we called to say that he was no longer safe to be at home, they told us that a bed was coming available later that day and that we should bring him in. So, on 17 February 2019, and for the seventh time in his life, dad was admitted to psychiatric hospital.

As was typical upon admission, after dad was given a full physical examination, a meeting was arranged to review his medication. Given our extensive experience of dad's treatment over what was now three decades, mum and I were invited to participate.

As he sat motionless in the corner of the room, dad was on two different antidepressants, plus an antipsychotic. It was clear to everyone in the room that none of the drugs were working, so I was pleased when the psychiatrist said that she would look at a new approach.

However, I was less enthused when she said that this new approach amounted to exchanging the antipsychotic for a different one, plus swapping one of his antidepressants for another one in the same class – called SSRIs – which target the neurotransmitter serotonin.

I'd already learnt from my research that people respond differently to the different classes of antidepressants, depending upon their genetically predetermined, autonomic type.

I knew that people who benefit from SSRIs have naturally strong sympathetic nerves, which make up one branch of the autonomic nervous system. However, it was already clear to me that dad wasn't one of these people. It was my belief that the opposing branch of his autonomic nervous system, the parasympathetic branch, was the dominant one. As a result, I believed that he would benefit from older, now out of favour, antidepressants, which target different neurotransmitters to serotonin.

In doing so, these older drugs boost the sympathetic nerves, bringing about balance in the autonomic nervous system, as Dr. Gellhorn had discovered 60 years earlier.

Chapter Eleven

IF MY understanding was right, I believed that dad's already strong parasympathetic nerves would be made even stronger by taking another antidepressant targeting serotonin. I feared that his autonomic nervous system would become even more imbalanced, making his mental health even worse. I left the meeting feeling deflated and returned to dad's room, where he promptly got on to the bed, faced the wall and tried to shut out his reality.

When I arrived home, I recounted the story to Pauline, who suggested that I should start a diary to record dad's progress during his hospital stay. In what turned out to be an inspired recommendation, I began a written, photographic and video diary, to document dad's mental health.

My first entry read,

17 FEBRUARY —
Irrational, very depressed, suicidal ideation.
MENTAL HEALTH SCORE (OUT OF 10) = 0

Word of dad's admission to hospital soon reached the anaesthetist who'd refused to administer the anaesthetic for dad's ECT. Despite dad's continued mental distress, he insisted that he wouldn't proceed with treatment before dad had undergone an ultrasound on his heart, as well as a CT scan.

Having begun his new medication, but still unable to recommence ECT, dad's mental state deteriorated.

24 FEBRUARY — Sat in corridor for most of day, very confused, hadn't showered or shaved.
MENTAL HEALTH SCORE = 0

25 FEBRUARY — Confused and rambling. Had to shower and shave him. Very fixed thinking, worried about being turfed out onto the street, no hope.
MENTAL HEALTH SCORE = 0

26 FEBRUARY — Same as yesterday.
MENTAL HEALTH SCORE = 0

27 FEBRUARY — No change, still very confused, low mood, tearful.
MENTAL HEALTH SCORE = 0

On 28 February, we received a letter from the hospital, confirming the date for dad's CT scan. 9 April. Nearly six weeks away. I couldn't believe it.

Evidently, nor could dad's psychiatrist, as she phoned her NHS colleagues to explain that he was a desperately ill patient on the psychiatric ward, requiring urgent attention. They responded to her plea with a revised date for his CT scan. 12 March. Dad had two weeks to hang on.

Two weeks later, on the morning of dad's scan, I received a phone call from mum.

"They've found two blood clots, one on each lung," she said.

Shaken by the news, I asked, "Is he going to be okay?"

"He's been taken to A&E and is there now. We don't have any further details, so we're just waiting to hear," she replied.

The A&E doctors flushed dad's lungs, then put him on blood thinners, before reporting to us that he was going to be okay. The CT scan, which had previously felt like a frustrating barrier to dad's treatment, had in all likelihood just saved his life. I felt so relieved, as well as indebted to the radiologist for spotting the clots, especially when the object of the investigation was his heart, not his lungs.

Dad spent the night under the observation of a mental health nurse, before returning to the psychiatric ward the following day, where I continued to document his mental condition.

14 MARCH — Worn out, very low mood, just getting by, staying on bed and having meals brought to him in room. Can't see a way through, bleak outlook.

MENTAL HEALTH SCORE = 0

Once visiting hours were over, just as I was about to say goodbye to dad, the psychiatrist entered his room. We reflected on the events of the past couple of days, then proceeded to discuss his treatment options. Given the discovery of the blood clots, we agreed that the anaesthetist was unlikely to give the go-ahead for ECT, so we needed an alternative.

She told me that she was considering another antidepressant, but needed financial approval before prescribing it. I was intrigued to know what class of antidepressant it was, to see whether it was likely to help balance his autonomic nervous system, or knock it further out of equilibrium.

When I asked for more details about the proposed drug, she took offence at my enquiry. After reminding me that she'd been a practising psychiatrist for 17 years, with a raised voice, she asked, "Would you like to manage your dad's mental health yourself?"

When I was posed this question, it was 43 years since I'd first seen dad suffering from depression. Over this period of time, he'd been hospitalised seven times, as well as having been given several hundred courses of electroconvulsive therapy and dozens of different psychiatric medications. With us sitting in dad's room, whilst he lay on the hospital bed with his eyes closed, unable to face the world, her invitation was too great an opportunity for me to ignore. I rushed home, knowing exactly where to begin. Gellhorn and Gonzalez. Reviewing my notes, I read,

Dr. Gellhorn - hospitalised psychiatric patients had a dysregulated autonomic nervous system, but when they had recovered from their mental illness, their autonomic nervous system was in homeostasis.

There are two branches to the autonomic nervous system, the sympathetic branch and the parasympathetic branch. Gellhorn's discovery told me that, to get dad out of hospital, I needed to balance these two systems. Through my extensive studies, I'd already identified that dad had a dominant parasympathetic branch, so I knew that to bring about equilibrium in his nervous system, I needed to boost the opposing one, the sympathetic branch. But how?

I reminded myself that the third element of Gonzalez's cancer protocol involved using diet and supplementation to bring about balance in the autonomic nervous system. I searched through my notes, looking for exact details of how he'd achieved it. Nothing. I found plenty of details about the theory, but no specifics on this third tier of his protocol.

I dusted off what I considered to be one of the best books I'd ever read, Gonzalez's *Nutrition and the Autonomic Nervous System*, hoping that I'd missed something when making my notes. I hadn't. Plenty of science, but no specifics on the treatment itself.

Dr. Gonzalez had passed away four years earlier so, fearful that his work had been lost to history, I scoured the internet, searching for an answer. After spending several unfruitful hours on Google, I discovered an obscure website containing a video of Gonzalez giving a four hour presentation to a group of doctors.

The first couple of hours contained information I already knew, including how he'd built on the work of Drs. Beard, Price, Pottenger, Funkenstein, Gellhorn and Kelley but, as the presentation entered the second half, my heart began to beat a little faster.

Over and over the video I went, pausing and rewinding to make sure I'd written down everything correctly. I found it difficult to contain my excitement, as Gonzalez provided specific details about what diet and supplements he'd given to his cancer patients, according to their autonomic type.

At the end of the video, I reviewed my notes, only to discover that – whilst I had plenty of details about the diet, as well as the names of the supplements – I didn't have anything about dosing, so I headed back to the internet.

There, I found a number of interviews he'd given which, whilst fascinating, didn't tell me what I needed. Feeling frustrated that I was so close to a potential solution, I reminded myself of what I'd done during my studies when facing a gap in my knowledge. I looked for a textbook containing the dosing information I needed.

After a few more hours of searching the internet, I discovered Dr. Abram Hoffer, a Canadian doctor who had successfully treated thousands of patients with schizophrenia, using nutrition and supplement therapy. Then, searching through the books he'd authored, I found a foreword he'd written for a book called *Natural Healing for Bipolar Disorder: A Compendium of Nutritional Approaches.* As I read the description, my pulse quickened. I knew I'd found what I'd been searching for,

"A state-of-the-art compendium, encompassing more than half a century of clinical experience and research by pioneering physicians worldwide. It describes the importance of each nutrient and herb to mental health, and depicts the major subtypes, their associated symptoms, chemistry, and vitamin needs."

When it arrived the following morning, I quickly opened the book to check whether it had the dosing information I required. It did. And for every supplement in Gonzalez's protocol.

Never before had I been so excited to open Microsoft Excel and through my adrenaline-fuelled fingers, I compiled a spreadsheet, with the name of the supplement in one column and the required dose in the next.

Once complete, I headed to the shops to buy what I needed to create my own protocol. Not to treat cancer, but depression.

When I returned home, I prepared the correct doses, then drove to the hospital to see dad, armed with a pill box filled with supplements. A few sips of water later, my new protocol had begun.

The following day, I woke up with a sense of nervousness. Although my treatment protocol involved starting on low doses, then increasing them over the course of a couple of weeks, I couldn't help but fantasise that I'd find dad feeling a bit better when I went to visit him later in the day.

My diary entry reads as follows:

16 MARCH — Definite slight improvement, eating better, immediately ate lots of home made granola that mum made, nurse said he'd been through to dining room and had given her a wave, more animated, calm, mood slightly better, smiling a bit, played dominos.
MENTAL HEALTH SCORE = 1

I couldn't quite believe it. Was it a coincidence, or was the protocol actually working?

Mum and I held our breath, reserving judgement until we saw how he'd be over the next few days.

17 MARCH — Similar to yesterday, showered and washed hair. Played dominos.
MENTAL HEALTH SCORE = 1

18 MARCH — Amazing day, drawing in the dining room when I arrived. Chatty, smiling, more relaxed and calm. Spoke of home and doing art at home. Nurse said he was chatty.

MENTAL HEALTH SCORE = 4

19 MARCH — Drawing again, started a new picture. He'd been chatting to OT nurse. Progress from yesterday sustained.

MENTAL HEALTH SCORE = 4

Then, the following day, he suffered a slight relapse.

20 MARCH – Not as bright as last two days, mum managed to get him into the garden, took an effort though.
MENTAL HEALTH SCORE = 2

I was worried that the progress we'd seen over the last few days wouldn't last. "Let's wait and see," mum said, trying to calm my fears.

21 MARCH – Definitely getting better. Brighter, smiles, bit of laughter, joking with the nurses, nurses report better appetite, shepherd's pie, wedges, beans on toast, large portion, nurse said he'd made witty comments to her. Can't see the progression himself yet.
MENTAL HEALTH SCORE = 4.5

22 MARCH – Really good, found him making milkshake in an OT session in the kitchen. Had been first to breakfast, had cereal and toast, nurse said he has been 'a different man since 16 March', much more chatty, eating better.
MENTAL HEALTH SCORE = 5

24 MARCH — Went out for a walk outside the hospital grounds for the first time, down to Maggie's! Played Scrabble. Chatting more.

MENTAL HEALTH SCORE = 5

As the doses of the supplements increased, we continued to see great progress. I was giddy with excitement. Then came his best day yet.

28 MARCH — A remarkable day, sooo much better, chatty, smiling, laughing. Mum, dad and I had a long chat, flowed easily, he can now see the progress and hopes that it continues. Went for a walk in the sunshine. Just amazing.

MENTAL HEALTH SCORE = 7.5

He had progressed so well that the staff agreed that he could go home for a couple of hours the following day.

29 MARCH — Went home for two hours, did really well, hospital has agreed to let him go home for four hours over the weekend.
MENTAL HEALTH SCORE = 7

30 MARCH — Four hours at home! Did really well, mood was good, determined to keep mobile to fight the Parkinson's.
MENTAL HEALTH SCORE = 7.5

31 MARCH — Home for six hours, firstly at mum and dad's, then came to watch the Liverpool v Tottenham game with me. Had Sunday lunch for Mother's Day, mood was great, good conversation.
MENTAL HEALTH SCORE = 7.5

Then, on 2 April 2019, dad was discharged from psychiatric hospital. For the first time in his entire life, he did so without the need for electroconvulsive therapy. In my diary, I scored his mental health as eight out of ten.

◊

It is now ten months since dad last had the treatment he'd been so reliant upon to maintain his mental health. Instead, he has natural supplements every day, plus a personalised diet. Since leaving hospital, he has been living at home with mum, just a few hundred yards from Pauline and me. Together, we do our best to help him battle Parkinson's disease.

Yesterday, over his favourite meal, we celebrated mum and dad's 54th wedding anniversary. As we sat around the table, we talked about the good times, as well as the many years of suffering. Dad thanked me for everything I'd done for him over that time. He said that he was eternally grateful to me for saving him from having ECT every fortnight, the treatment he'd been afraid might cost him his life.
His words of gratitude prompted me to reflect, not only on the remarkable events of the last few months but also on the first half of my life, before I'd identified my true calling. The years I'd spent pursuing my fortune, firstly in London, then running my own business, had provided me with thrills, but no real meaning. It wasn't until I'd turned fully towards dad's suffering and allowed myself to be led by the compass of my heart that I discovered my true purpose in life. I looked back at dad and with tears of redemption in my eyes I replied, "No dad, you saved me."

Epilogue

I wrote this book for several reasons. Firstly, in telling dad's story, I wanted to acknowledge his courage in successfully battling an illness which has lasted for over four decades. And without mum's care over 54 years of marriage, I don't know how the story would have ended, so my second tribute is for her unwavering love and support.

I also wanted to speak up for the many people around the world who suffer with mental illness, some of whom may be struggling whilst they read this book. If this is you, I want you to know that there is hope. If dad's story tells only one thing, then it is that recovery is possible, even in the most difficult of circumstances.

Lastly, I wanted to demonstrate that there is another way to treat mental illness. I believe that we owe it to all the sufferers around the world to further explore how balancing the autonomic nervous system resolves this disease. I hope that somewhere, someone reading this book is in a position to further advance this inquiry.

About Matt

In serving his true calling, Matt now works with companies and individuals, helping them to achieve great mental health and to discover their own purpose in life.

For individuals

Together with Pauline, Matt runs retreats for people looking to transform their lives and their wellbeing. For more details, visit wearepencil.co.uk

For companies

Using his understanding of the brain and body, and how to fuel them properly, Matt provides advice on how to achieve exceptional mental health and productivity in the workplace. For further information, visit mattjanes.com

For everyone

Matt's free online course is available at thethrivecourse.com

Glossary

Autonomic nervous system – A series of nerves which connects to every tissue, organ and gland in the body, but over which we have no conscious control. The autonomic nervous system consists of two branches – the sympathetic nervous system and the parasympathetic nervous system. Each produces an opposing effect on the body. The two branches work in reciprocity, meaning that when one dials up, the other dials down.

Sympathetic nervous system – The 'fight or flight' branch of the autonomic nervous system is concerned with our short term survival and is activated in the body's stress response. In fact, any movement of any kind, from reading to running, mobilises the sympathetic nervous system.

Parasympathetic nervous system – The regeneration branch of the autonomic nervous system, which takes care of long term survival issues, including the activation of our immune system, as well as the repair and rebuilding of our organs and tissues. Whilst the sympathetic branch needs to become mobilised for us to fight, or run from danger, the parasympathetic branch must do so for us to recover from any resulting injury. Sometimes referred to as the 'rest and digest' branch, the parasympathetic system must become activated for us to sleep, as well as digest food.

Homeostasis – The state which is achieved when the two branches of the autonomic nervous system are in balance. This is the state Dr. Gellhorn observed when his psychiatric patients recovered from their illnesses.

The two branches of the autonomic nervous system also need to work together for us to successfully go about our daily lives. For example, whilst the sympathetic nervous system must activate for us to prepare food, the parasympathetic nervous system must mobilise for us to digest it properly. This goes some way to explaining why, when we're stressed and our sympathetic nervous system is in overdrive, we can experience stomach ache or an upset tummy after a meal (because the sympathetic branch is activated, instead of the parasympathetic branch we actually need).

The same balance needs to be in place when we go to bed. Whilst the night time ritual of brushing our teeth requires our sympathetic nervous system, in order to carry out the activity, our parasympathetic nervous system needs to mobilise for us to sleep. This helps to explain why we struggle to sleep when we're stressed; we have an over-active sympathetic nervous system.

Everyone has different degrees of (genetically determined) balance in their autonomic nervous system. Some people, like dad, have a dominant parasympathetic nervous system and, as a result, are susceptible to depression. To achieve balance, and good mental health, this group of people need to stimulate the opposing branch, the sympathetic nervous system. In dad's case, I achieved this by using a carefully designed protocol of natural supplements, restoring balance (homeostasis) in his autonomic nervous system.

This is the same explanation for how electroconvulsive therapy helps to temporarily relieve dad of his depression. ECT stimulates the sympathetic nerves, bringing about autonomic balance in people who are genetically 'parasympathetic dominant'. This helps to explain why ECT doesn't work for everyone who suffers from depression; people with strong sympathetic nerves don't need this branch further stimulating. Instead, they need to calm this branch and instead boost the parasympathetic branch of their autonomic nervous system to restore health.

Other groups of people have a naturally dominant sympathetic nervous system. Under stress, this group can suffer from anxiety because their strong sympathetic nerves are further stimulated by whatever is causing them distress. Such people benefit from a different set of supplements to calm their sympathetic nerves and boost their parasympathetic nerves, to bring about autonomic balance.

For further information, visit mattjanes.com